Royal Navy Battleships

1895-1946

W. D. G. Blundell

ALMARK PUBLISHING CO. LTD., LONDON

First published — February 1973

ISBN 0 85524 092 X (hard cover edition)
ISBN 0 85324 093 8 (paper covered edition)

By the same author in this series:
Ships of the Royal Navy
Royal Navy Warships, 1939–1945
German Navy Warships, 1939–1945

Printed in Great Britain by
Martins Press Ltd., London EC1R 0EN
for the publishers, Almark Publishing Co. Ltd.,
270 Burlington Road, New Malden,
Surrey KT3 4NL, England.

Introduction

THIS book provides a comprehensive coverage of all battleships that served in the Royal Navy from 1895 onwards and, as this type of warship has long since passed out of service, is a historical document that describes the ships in an easily readable manner. Each ship, or class of ship, is illustrated by constant scale drawings to the popular 'international' scale of 1 : 1200 (100 feet to the inch). In addition photographs of most ships are included and these, combined with the drawings, give a good visual impression of each ship. The photographs, most of them previously unpublished, have been selected primarily for clarity and detail rather than artistic effect. It is hoped that this book will appeal equally to warship enthusiasts, naval war-gamers and warship modellers. Using the plans herein, for instance, it would be possible to build up a complete miniature fleet in 1 : 1200 scale using balsa or hardwood on the usual 'layer by layer' principle for constructing small-scale model ships.

The drawings and photographs are accompanied by brief notes pointing out salient features of design and history, plus basic data in standardized form giving (in order) displacement, overall length and beam, armament, maximum speed and complement. An introductory chapter describes the developments in construction, political factors, and the operational uses of battleships in both World Wars. At the beginning of this century, and for over three hundred years before, the battleship reigned supreme over the oceans and no maritime power could afford to be without such ships. Then, with the dawning of air power, their awesome size and armament slowly became impotent until they are now nothing but a memory. (The USA still retains four such ships in reserve and recently one of them, **New Jersey,** was used as a fire support ship in Vietnam.)

For their kind help and assistance, especially with photographs, grateful acknowledgement is made to the Ministry of Defence (Navy), DG Ships, Section 423C, and the Imperial War Museum. T. G. Royall has also kindly provided pictures from his collection.

CONTENTS

HMS Marlborough *of the 'Iron Duke' class, Britain's most modern type of battleship at the start of World War 1. These were the first British oil-burning battleships though initially they were also coal-fired. This picture dates from 1918 and shows the lighter grey adopted for Royal Navy ships in home waters—previously they had been dark grey (IWM).*

FRONT COVER: A colour print of HMS Canopus *taken from an early colour post-card of 1906 (T. G. Royall collection). The lower picture shows HMS* Dreadnought *entering Portsmouth Harbour in 1914—the ship which gave its name to the big gun battleship, a prime naval weapon of World War 1 (IWM-Q21183).*

Historical Development

BEFORE 1895

FOR over three hundred years, from the beginning of the seventeenth century until the middle of World War 2, the battleship—or line of battleship as it was called in days of sail—was the solid backbone of any navy. Without a strong navy no maritime country could hope to expand or prosper from overseas territories which she had an interest or foothold in. Although other types of warships were introduced, generally lighter and faster, it was still the battleship —carrying the heaviest armament afloat—that did and would settle the final affair. This maxim still held good when sail and wood were replaced by steam and steel in the last half of the nineteenth century.

Britain, the world's greatest maritime power for centuries and possessor of the largest empire, knew she had a sure shield in the Royal Navy. In turn, to continue to be effective, the Royal Navy had to lead world warship design and certainly had to have more and better battleships than any other country. In 1859 the **Warrior** was laid down and became the first warship in the world to be constructed of iron from the keel up. Other developments quickly followed, which included more powerful engines, the disappearance of sail, and larger guns mounted in revolving turrets. Each successive ship was nearly always an individual design incorporating improvements and, consequently, although some groups of ships were called classes this was a misnomer as they differed considerably in layout and armament. With the **Majestic** class of 1895 uniformity was attained for the first time and it is to these ships, and their successors, that we now turn.

PRE-DREADNOUGHTS

The year 1895 has been chosen for the starting point of this book because by then battleship design had settled down to a similar standard for all navies. For the next decade all Royal Navy battleships, and most of their contemporaries in foreign navies, carried 4×12 inch guns as a main armament. These guns were mounted in two turrets and were supplemented by a secondary armament, for use against torpedo boats and destroyers, of smaller quick-firing guns. Towards the end of this decade an intermediate battery of quite large guns, 9·2 inch calibre, was introduced on some ships. However, this was not popular, due to confusion over spotting the fall of shot, and was only a short-lived phase. Another typical feature, that was to remain inherent in battleship design until the end of World War 1, was the ram type bow. The influencing factor for the retention of this last resort weapon had been the Battle of Lissa, fought between the Austro-Hungarian and Italian fleets in 1866, where it had been used effectively and caused more damage than gunfire. Anti-torpedo nets, of steel wire, were carried and lowered along the sides of ships to protect them when laying at anchor. Triple expansion engines of 17–18,000 HP gave,

Typical of the early iron-clad line-of-battle ships was HMS Anson, *shown here in 1893. The guns are in open barbettes and the ships were much smaller than the new 'Majestic' class which appeared the same year. (IWM-Q38128)*

on average, a top speed of 18 knots. Displacing around 15,000 tons, this was to remain the standard type of battleship for ten years.

In October 1906 HMS **Dreadnought** was completed, having been built in the record time of one year and in as much secrecy as possible, and every other battleship in the world became obsolete. Such was the influence of the **Dreadnought's** revolutionary design—10 × 12 inch guns and turbines giving 22 knots—that all earlier battleships were re-classified as 'pre-Dreadnoughts'. With only four large guns and 18 knots speed they were neither powerful enough to fight nor fast enough to escape from what was now to become the standard type of battleship. Germany, France, the USA and many smaller countries had to drastically revise their battleship building programmes to keep pace with Britain.

BATTLE CRUISERS

Although not covered in this book brief mention must be made, at this stage, of the battle cruiser concept which appeared soon after the **Dreadnought**. (A separate book on this type of warship has been published.*) As in the case of the **Dreadnought** this type was the idea of Admiral 'Jackie' Fisher, Britain's

British Battle Cruisers, by Peter C Smith (Almark)

Chief of Naval Staff for several years in the early twentieth century, to whom the Royal Navy owed so much for its revolutionary progress. The battle cruiser concept was, in theory, perfect. Here was a ship that mounted almost the main armament of a battleship—only one gun turret less—and had a much higher speed—at least 4 to 5 knots faster. To attain such high speed much more powerful machinery had to be incorporated which resulted in these ships being longer than contemporary battleships. However, in order to obtain both these highly desirable qualities, something had to be sacrificed and that was adequate protective armour plating. Even from the beginning this weak point was acknowledged but, it was argued, with her high speed the battle cruiser could always avoid action. Such a ship could sink any inferior warship and stay out of the range of a battleship's guns.

These theories were borne out at the Battle of The Falkland Islands, in December 1914, when the **Invincible** and **Inflexible** destroyed the German South Pacific Squadron consisting of armoured and light cruisers. Unfortunately, as the war progressed, they were employed as the spearhead of the British Fleet and had to bear the brunt of the fighting. This was tragically illustrated at the Battle of Jutland, in May 1916, when the battle cruisers were forced to engage German battleships. Their weak armour plating proved fatal and three of them, **Queen Mary, Indefatigable** and **Invincible,** were blown up with tremendous loss of life. Twenty-five years later almost to the day, in May 1941, the same sad lesson was to be re-learnt with the terrible loss of the **Hood** in action with the German battleship **Bismarck.**

DREADNOUGHTS

After the **Dreadnought** had entered service the international battleship building race was on and the principal contestants were Britain and Germany. Whatever happened, as far as Britain was concerned, Germany must never be

On the bridge of a 'Majestic class battleship in about 1898. The ship was in harbour and only the duty watch of signalmen are present. The charthouse (in teak finish) is to the left, and the magnetic compass binnacle is in the centre. Signal flag lockers are to the right Note the semaphore signal post in the background and the searchlight in the bridge wings.

ABOVE: HMS Dreadnought 'Cleared for Action' on exercises in 1907. Note the 12-pdr quick firers (anti-torpedo boat guns) on the top of the turret, the gunlayers' sighting ports, the windlass abaft the nearest turret, and the rum-issuing containers by the mast. When cleared away, all guardrails, stanchions, and posts, were dropped to give a clear arc of fire for the guns. BELOW: The old battleship Cornwallis firing on the Turks after the Gallipoli evacuation, December 20, 1915. She was the last Allied ship to leave Suvla Bay. Note the anti-torpedo nets rigged on their folding booms from the ship's side, to port. On the starboard side they are folded in. Also to starboard is rigged a lower boom to which were secured ship's boats while at anchor (IWM-Q13682).

The pre-Dreadnought Agamemnon *at Mudros in 1915 when taking part in the Dardanelles campaign. Note the early style of disruptive camouflage, mainly using white and light grey paint. A false bow wave is a feature. Wind scoops (of canvas) are rigged above hatches on the forecastle to direct fresh air down hatchways to the mess decks. Main topmast is struck, and torpedo nets are fully rigged. These were topped up to the ship's side and the nets stowed away when the ship went to sea (IWM-SP67).*

allowed to catch up, for with her ever-growing overseas ambitions she was now recognized as the potential enemy. Following the **Dreadnought** came the six ships of the **Bellerophon** and **St. Vincent** classes which were basically similar to the earlier ship. An increased secondary armament—4 inch guns instead of 12 pounders—was mounted but, like the **Dreadnought,** they could only bring eight of their main guns to bear on a broadside due to their turret arrangement. This was rectified in the next three ships by mounting the wing turrets in echelon and placing 'X' turret higher than 'Y' (the rear two turrets). All these ships had 12 inch guns for their main armament and, with the exception of the **Agincourt** mentioned later, were the only post-Dreadnoughts to do so.

With the next three classes of twelve ships, **Orion, King George V** and **Iron Duke,** the main armament was increased to 13·5 inch guns all mounted on the centre line to enable a full broadside to be fired. This increased the length and displacement of these ships, which were all similar in design and layout, and more powerful machinery had to be installed to maintain a speed of 21–22 knots. The **Iron Duke** class re-introduced the 6 inch gun as secondary armament; this calibre gun had not been used in battleships since the pre-Dreadnoughts, and were the first British warships to mount anti-aircraft guns when they were built.

Three other battleships, which did not fit into the general scheme of construction, nearing completion in British shipyards were taken over by the

Irresistible *passing a tow to* Albion *after the latter had grounded while shelling Turkish positions at Gaba Tepe in the Dardanelles. Note the white mark on deck which indicates an area to be kept clear around the after windlass and capstan. At left the tow rope and anchor cable is flaked on deck ready for passing to the towing ship (IWM-Q13806).*

Royal Navy just before World War One. These ships were:
Agincourt originally ordered for Brazil and then re-ordered for Turkey, main armament was 14 × 12 inch guns.
Erin originally ordered for Turkey, main armament was 10 × 13·5 inch guns.
Canada originally ordered for Chile, main armament was 10 × 14 inch guns.

FIRST WORLD WAR

At the start of the war Britain had 65 battleships, including 25 Dreadnoughts. This was an impressive total compared with Germany which had 37, of which 17 were Dreadnoughts. Nearing completion were the five ships of the **Queen Elizabeth** class and construction had already begun on five ships of the **Royal Sovereign** class. These ten ships were to be larger, faster and more heavily armed than any of the previous classes. They were to be armed with 8 × 15 inch guns, in four turrets of two, and would introduce oil-fired boilers to battleships. If the much smaller German battle fleet dared to venture forth into the North Sea, against this powerful opposition, then it would probably be destroyed. However, Germany could not have built her own sizeable fleet for no operational purpose, and sooner or later there would have to be a major engagement.

Offensive sweeps and patrols were carried out in the North Sea by the British from the commencement of hostilities but there was to be no clash of the

Irresistible *herself became a victim of war in the Dardanelles. Here she is sinking after being torpedoed in 1915. This loss showed the great vulnerability of the slower, older battleships and led to their early withdrawal from major operations (IWM-020375).*

giants, on the scale imagined, for nearly two years, although there were other naval engagements. The battleships were not present at the Heligoland Bight engagement in August 1914, in which three German cruisers were sunk, as this only involved the battle cruisers and lighter warships. At the Battle of The Falkland Islands, in December 1914, battle cruisers were again in action and also were present at the Battle of The Dogger Bank, in January 1915, where the German armoured cruiser **Blücher** was sunk. A use was found for several of the old pre-Dreadnoughts and the new **Queen Elizabeth** when the Dardanelles campaign started in February 1915. Here they were able to put their main armament to good use, to give fire support to the invasion forces, in the coastal bombardment role. However, after five of the older ships had been sunk by means of mines, torpedoes and shore gunfire, these were hastily withdrawn.

Towards the end of May 1916, both the German and British fleets were at sea in considerable force and, at long last, were destined to meet. On the afternoon of May 31 the British battle cruisers, well in advance of the main battle fleet, sighted their opposite numbers in the German Navy. Turning on to a south-easterly course the German battle cruisers lured the advance British ships towards their battle fleet and, during this chase, firing commenced. When the German battle fleet was sighted the British battle cruisers, playing the same game as their counterparts, turned on to a reciprocal course to bring the enemy battle fleet into contact with the British battle fleet. This was accomplished just after 6 pm, and both fleets opened fire. For over two hours

The old battleship Triumph *in the Dardanelles. This campaign was the main naval operation involving pre-Dreadnoughts in World War 1. The cranes of* Triumph *(and her sister* Swiftsure*) were a distinctive feature of these two ships which were originally built for a foreign power (IWM-SP2456).*

the great ships exchanged fire on an easterly course and then, with poor visibility due to mist, gun smoke and night falling, contact was lost. Admiral Jellicoe pursued until the early hours of the following morning when he decided, mainly because of the risk of entering German minefields in the dark, to turn north and return to Scapa Flow.

Controversy has raged ever since this battle and both sides have claimed it as a victory. British losses were heavier and comprised of three battle cruisers, three armoured cruisers and eight destroyers as opposed to one battle cruiser, one pre-Dreadnought, four light cruisers and eight destroyers. Battle damage to

BELOW: The battleships of the Grand Fleet, seen at sea in 1916, just before Jutland, made up the most powerful force of sea power then known. 'Iron Duke' class ships are in the nearest column (IWM-Q18121).

surviving German ships was more extensive. Only one British battleship was badly damaged, the **Marlborough,** which was hit by a torpedo but managed to reach port under her own steam.

After the Battle of Jutland the German battle fleet never put to sea again in force, except for a brief sortie in August 1916, when they returned to base immediately when it was learnt that the British battle fleet was at sea, and all future warship construction was concentrated on U-boats. If Jellicoe had pursued the Germans he could have so easily lost his battleships in the mine-fields and, had this happened, Britain would have lost control of the sea and eventually the war. Jellicoe had to keep the fleet intact, 'the fleet in being', to enable Britain to have dominant sea power—the very existence of the battle fleet was, at that period, the great deterrent—It would have been an extremely reckless commander, to decide on the spot with the limited information available, who ordered the pursuit to be carried on. Jellicoe has been criticized by many people with the wisdom of hindsight, but there can be but little doubt that he had made the correct decision.

For the rest of the war naval activity was centred around the submarines on which Germany staked so much. Although heavy losses were inflicted on Allied merchant shipping this menace was gradually overcome by the re-introduction of the convoy system, last used over a century before in the Napoleonic Wars, and increased numbers of escorting warships. When the USA entered the war, in 1917, victory for the Allies was assured. Nine new American battleships joined the already powerful British battle fleet which gave an overwhelming superiority. In November 1918, the German battle fleet went to sea for the last time and were escorted, by the Royal Navy, to Scapa Flow. Seven months later they were scuttled by their crews and the world's second largest navy ceased to exist.

As a result of war experience many lessons were learnt and alterations and modifications made of which the following were the most important:

(a) The removal of non-essential top hamper, such as stern walks, high top-masts and other equipment that was subject to blast effect.

The 15-inch guns roar out in a mighty broadside from HMS Royal Sovereign, *on battle exercises in 1918. The 'Royal Sovereign' class were the latest battleships in service at that time (IWM-Q17991).*

(*b*) The change over from coal- to oil-firing boilers.
(*c*) Additional ready use life-saving equipment in the form of Carley floats.
(*d*) Anti-torpedo bulges were fitted and the old net defence was removed.
(*e*) Paravanes, for cutting the cables of moored mines, were fitted.
(*f*) Searchlights and visual signalling equipment were improved.
(*g*) It was finally realized that the ram type of bows was a waste of time and would not be incorporated into future ships.
(*h*) Spotting aircraft were carried and operated off flight platforms mounted on gun turrets and extending over the guns.
(*i*) Anti-aircraft guns were added and also deck protection was increased in case of bombing attacks.

BETWEEN THE WARS

With 'the war to end wars' over the popular theme, not unnaturally, was disarmament for all the great powers. In the early 1920s nearly all the surviving British battleships, with the exception of the ten ships of the **Queen Elizabeth** and **Royal Sovereign** classes, were scrapped quickly or were used as training ships. Of the pre-war battleships only the **Iron Duke** and **Centurion** were destined to serve in World War 2 in secondary roles. The Washington Naval Treaty limited the size of capital ships to 35,000 tons, and in the case of Germany 10,000 tons, which accounted for the unusual design of the only two battleships that Britain completed before World War 2. (See under **Nelson** and **Rodney**.)

For many years the general naval opinion held that the battleship still remained the supreme weapon at sea. Admittedly it had been practically demonstrated that a battleship could be sunk by an aircraft but this had been, it was argued, against a stationary ship with no defence. A modern battleship at high speed, taking evasive action and with an adequate anti-aircraft armament was extremely unlikely to be sunk by aircraft. There was a more definite risk of loss by submarine attack but this, however, could be considerably reduced by means of destroyer screens. Aircraft did have their use though, even to the most resolute of the old school, for scouting and spotting for the guns. Consequently nearly all the battleships were fitted with aircraft catapults, handling cranes and seaplanes for these purposes. Increased deck protection and additional anti-aircraft guns were fitted to all ships and, from the **Nelson** and **Rodney** onwards, any future ships would have these features built into them.

By the mid-1930s another world war seemed unavoidable, and the major powers had to start thinking about battleship construction once more. Germany already had five modern capital ships and was building at least two more. Although three of these ships were 'pocket' battleships—armed with 6×11 inch guns on only 10,000 tons displacement—all these ships were faster than any British battleship of that time. Further afield Italy was building faster battleships and Japan, shrouded in secrecy but recognized as a fast-growing menace, was certainly building some big and fast warships. (These turned out to be the **Yamato** and **Musashi,** the world's biggest battleships ever, of over 64,000 tons with 9×18 inch guns.) France had built two new battle cruisers, which were almost fast battleships in many respects, and had another two under construction. Across the Atlantic the USA had started to build fast ships armed with 9×16 inch guns. With only 12 battleships, 10 of them of World War One vintage, and all of them with a low top speed Britain had to start building again fast to catch up with the rest of the world. The result was the five ships of the **King George V** class being laid down but, before any of these were completed, World War 2 had begun.

WORLD WAR TWO

No action ever took place on the lines visualized, mainly from World War 1 experience, of opposing battle fleets fighting it out on the grand scale as at the Battle of Jutland. Germany did not concentrate her few battleships together but chose to use them, in the early stages of the war, as individual surface raiders operating against merchant shipping. In this role, on the rare sorties that were made, some of the German ships were highly successful and certainly forced the British to provide a battleship escort for major convoys. When Italy entered the war, in 1940, her battleships outnumbered the British battle fleet that was

HMS Barham *(centre) with the carrier* Ark Royal, *and battlecruiser* Renown *in the Mediterranean in February 1941. In World War 2 opportunities to employ battleships against enemy fleets were rare and they were used mainly as fire support or escort ships (IWM-A27239).*

15

All the British battleships were modernized to a degree either before or during World War 2. This view of HMS Ramillies *in May 1943 shows typical changes; radar aerials at mast heads, radar aerials on directors, small AA guns on turret, 4-inch twin high angle guns, and bulges, all alterations to the basic design. Note the false ship outline in the camouflage pattern on the ship's side (MoD).*

available in the Mediterranean. These odds were quickly reduced by a night attack on the naval base at Taranto, by Swordfish aircraft from the aircraft carrier **Illustrious,** when half the Italian battle fleet was sunk or badly damaged by aerial torpedoes. This action was, without any doubt, the beginning of the demise of the battleship as the supreme weapon of sea power and marked the ascent of the aircraft carrier. However, it was to be much later before this changing aspect was fully recognized.

Perhaps the nearest approach to an action of the, by now, old-fashioned type came at the Battle of Matapan in 1941. Whilst in pursuit of a powerful Italian squadron the Mediterranean battle fleet, comprising of the **Warspite, Barham** and **Valiant,** sunk three Italian heavy cruisers at night. However, even in this action, the real trap had been laid by naval aircraft damaging one of the enemy ships earlier in the day and reducing her speed; the other two ships had remained behind the main force to escort her. During the **Bismarck** action several British battleships had inflicted severe damage but, once again, the enemy's fate had been sealed by naval torpedo bombers reducing her speed. For over two years Britain had borne the brunt of the naval war but now two more of the world's greatest powers were to enter the conflict.

On December 7, 1941, Japan, without a declaration of war, attacked the American naval base at Pearl Harbor. Within two hours the US Pacific battle fleet was either sunk or badly damaged by Japanese carrier-based aircraft. Although these ships were at anchor, as in the case of Taranto, any further doubts about battleship supremacy were to be dispelled a few days later. Steaming at high speed, and carrying out evasive action, the new battleship **Prince of Wales** with the battle cruiser **Repulse** were sunk by Japanese aircraft off the East coast of Malaya. There was no doubt now, in anyone's mind, that the battleship could not operate without effective air cover. This could only be provided by aircraft carriers but much more important, it was realized, was that these ships extended the range of a fleet's offensive weapons hundreds of miles over the horizon which had been the practical limit of a battleship's guns. The Battle of Midway and the subsequent Pacific actions demonstrated this vividly and the battleship had been, in practice, relegated to a heavy escort ship for fast carrier task forces.

Britain appreciated the new role that battleships would play and cancelled the projected **Lion** class, thus enabling more of her warship building yards to concentrate on aircraft carriers. (This class was to be an enlarged version of the **King George V** class, in many respects, displacing over 40,000 tons and armed with 9×16 inch guns.) Only one more battleship was to be built, the **Vanguard** mounting eight old 15 inch guns, and this was completed after the war. As aircraft carriers became more plentiful the battleship's spotting aircraft, and associated equipment, were removed to allow for extra crew accommodation and more light anti-aircraft guns to be fitted.

A sole exception, of aircraft not taking part in a battleship action, was when the **Duke of York** destroyed the **Scharnhorst** north of the Arctic Circle in the winter of 1943. Several of the older battleships provided the heavy escort for major convoys throughout the war and, equally important, gave heavy gun support for the Allies' invasions of Europe in Italy and Normandy. When the British Pacific Fleet was formed, to help the US Navy in this theatre of operations, the faster battleships of the **King George V** class acted as the heavy escorts for the carrier task force. In the Pacific the Japanese battleships were all sunk, mainly by naval aircraft, through not being able to have adequate air cover.

AFTER WORLD WAR TWO

Once again another war had ended and once again the ideal of all the major powers was to disarm as quickly as possible. Japan, Germany and Italy were finished as countries with large navies and Russia, at best a suspicious ally, was primarily a land power. These factors plus the atomic bomb and the battleship's obvious decline in importance led to an early scrapping, by most countries, of their battleships which were expensive to maintain and required large crews to man them.

In Britain all the pre-war ships were scrapped within three years of the war's end. (There was talk of preserving the **Warspite,** veteran of Jutland and Matapan but, unfortunately, nothing ever came of it.) A big question mark hung over the **King George V** class and **Vanguard,** for many years, as to their possible use. Some US Navy battleships were used in the Korean War, 1950–53, for coastal bombardment but no British battleship was to ever fire a shot in anger again. Towards the end of the 1950s the remaining five battleships had no place in the contracting Royal Navy and were scrapped, thus marking the end of a long era.

Index to Ships and Classes

Each class name ship, where appropriate, is in **bold** type and preceded by the year(s) of construction. As there were two distinct types of battleships, pre-Dreadnoughts and Dreadnoughts, the list of contents has been divided accordingly.

PRE-DREADNOUGHTS

DREADNOUGHTS

Prince George MoD *c. 1900*

1895–98
MAJESTIC, MAGNIFICENT, HANNIBAL, PRINCE GEORGE, VICTORIOUS, JUPITER, MARS, CAESAR, ILLUSTRIOUS

14,900 tons
413' OA × 75'
4 × 12 inch, 12 × 6 inch, 16 × 12 pdr, 12 × 3 pdr, 5 × 18 inch TT
Triple Expansion, 12,000 HP, 17½ knots
757

THIS was the first class of battleship to attain uniformity following the introduction of steel-built ships. They introduced the twin 12 inch gun turret, which fully enclosed the gun breeches and handling machinery; prior to this the main armament had been mounted on open barbettes which gave no protection to the guns' crews. With their two funnels mounted side by side, as opposed to the usual fore and aft in later ships, they were quite distinctive. Well before World War 1 they were all obsolete but were, nevertheless, used for various operations.

Two of this class, **Majestic** and **Prince George**, took part in the Dardanelles campaign and it was there that the **Majestic** was torpedoed and sunk by the U21 in 1915. This was to be the only war casualty of the class as most of the others, except **Jupiter** and **Caesar** which were retained in their roles and served overseas, were disarmed and served in minor roles as depot ships, transports and store ships. The guns from **Magnificent, Victorious, Mars** and **Illustrious** were mounted on eight monitors and used for coastal bombardment. Between 1919 and 1923 the remaining eight ships were sold and scrapped.

![Victorious stern photograph]

Victorious (stern)   *c. 1898*

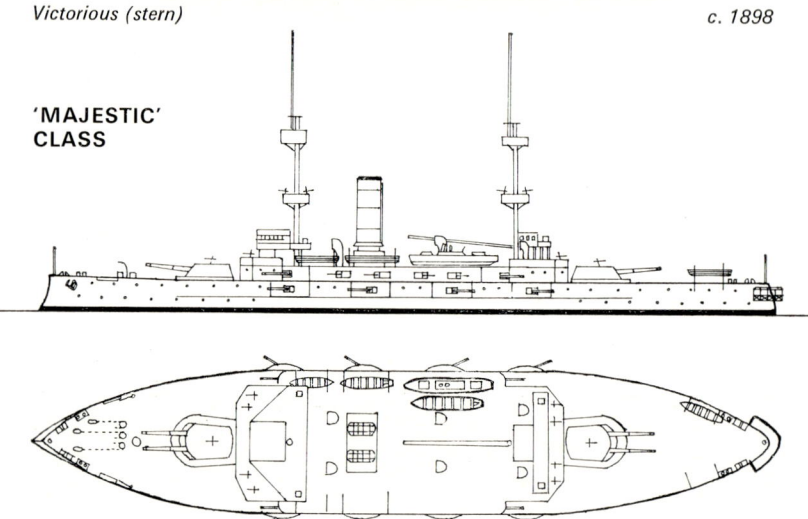

**'MAJESTIC'
CLASS**

Illustrious   MoD   c. 1908

Prince George   MoD   1897

Glory (stern) MoD 1/1901

1897–99
CANOPUS, GOLIATH, ALBION, OCEAN, GLORY, VENGEANCE

12,950 tons
418' OA × 74'
4 × 12 inch, 12 × 6 inch, 10 × 12 pdr, 6 × 3 pdr, 4 × 18 inch TT
Triple Expansion, 13,500 HP, 18 knots
750

THIS class introduced a layout that became almost standard for most of the later classes of pre-Dreadnoughts. Slightly longer than the earlier **Majestic**

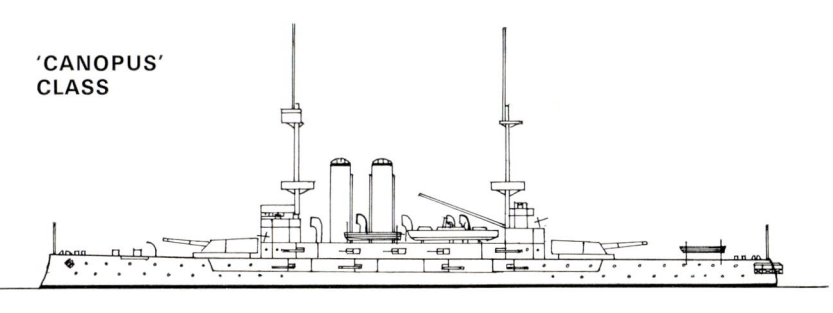

**'CANOPUS'
CLASS**

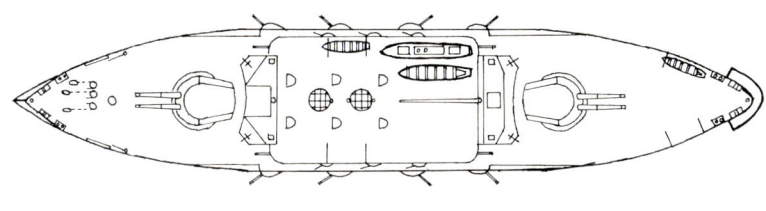

Ocean   *MoD*   *1900*

23

Canopus   MoD   2/1900

class they incorporated more powerful engines and improved boilers which raised their speed slightly. Once again, at the outbreak of World War 1, they were obsolete like all pre-Dreadnoughts but gave useful service and two of them were sunk in action.

Had it not been for her slow speed the **Canopus** might well have been involved in the operations against the German South Pacific Squadron which resulted in the Battles of Coronel and The Falkland Islands. During this period she acted as Guardship at The Falkland Islands in case the German Squadron tried to capture this British colony. After this the whole class, except the **Glory,** took part in the Dardanelles campaign. It was there that two ships were lost—the **Goliath** was torpedoed and the **Ocean** was sunk by a mine and gunfire. By the end of the war the surviving four had become depot ships and were scrapped between 1919 and 1922. (The **Glory** was renamed **Crescent** in 1919 and was the last of this class to be scrapped.)

Goliath   MoD   1900

Canopus   T. G. Royall   7/1906

Formidable　　　　　　　　　　　MoD　　　　　　　　　　　1900

1899
FORMIDABLE, IRRESISTIBLE, IMPLACABLE

15,000 tons
430' OA × 75'
4 × 12 inch, 12 × 6 inch, 16 × 12 pdr, 6 × 3 pdr, 6 × 18 inch TT
Triple Expansion, 15,000 HP, $18\frac{1}{2}$ knots
780

SLIGHTLY larger than the preceding class these ships introduced the 12 inch 40 calibre gun—earlier ships mounted 35 calibre. (The number of calibres denoted the length of a gun multiplied by its diameter. For example, a 40 calibre 12 inch gun was 40 × 12 inch or 40 feet from breech to muzzle.) The number of 12 pdr guns was increased and more powerful engines raised the top speed slightly. Obsolete before World War 1, only one of this class was to survive that conflict.

The **Formidable** was torpedoed and sunk by the U24 in the English Channel during 1915. Whilst taking part in the Dardanelles campaign in 1915, the **Irresistible** was mined and sunk by shore batteries. Taking part in the same campaign the **Implacable** survived to assist the Italian Fleet blockade the Austrian Fleet and, for this purpose, she was based at Taranto. In 1918 she formed part of the warship force on Northern patrol duties and was scrapped three years later.

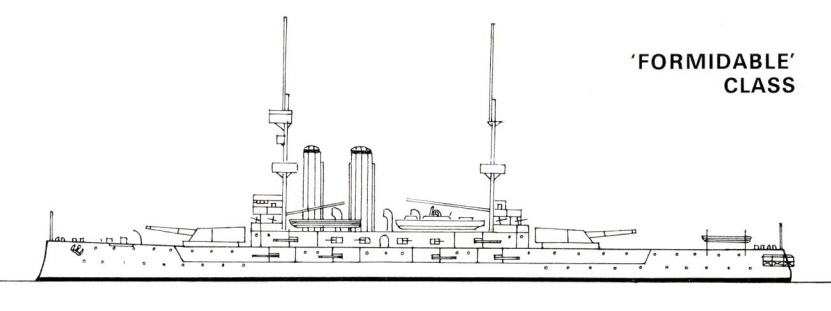

Implacable   MoD   c. 1901

'FORMIDABLE'
CLASS

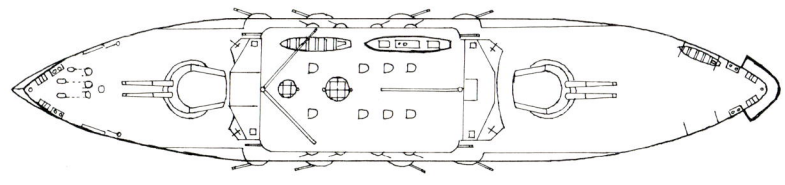

27

Bulwark   *MoD*   *1901*

1899
LONDON, BULWARK, VENERABLE
15,000 tons
430' OA × 75'
4 × 12 inch, 12 × 6 inch, 16 × 12 pdr, 6 × 3 pdr, 4 × 18 inch TT
Triple Expansion, 15,000 HP, 18 knots
780

EXTERNALLY there was little difference between the **London** and **Formidable** classes but internally the former had a longer belt of armour amidships. At one stage in their career, before World War One, these ships carried two large launches each of which were capable of firing torpedoes.

Just before World War 1 started the **Bulwark** was destroyed by an internal explosion which was not due, as far as is known, to enemy action. Although not employed as first-line battleships both the remaining ships continued to give useful service during the war. The **London** was based in Taranto as part of the force that blockaded the Austrian Fleet. After this she acted as a minelayer, in 1918, for a short while before becoming a depot ship at the end of the war; in 1920 she was scrapped. In the early stages of the war, before the specialized monitors became available, the **Venerable** acted in the coastal bombardment role off the Belgian coast. In 1915 she was sent to the Mediterranean where the rest of the war was spent. Like many other pre-Dreadnoughts she became a depot ship for a while before scrapping in 1920.

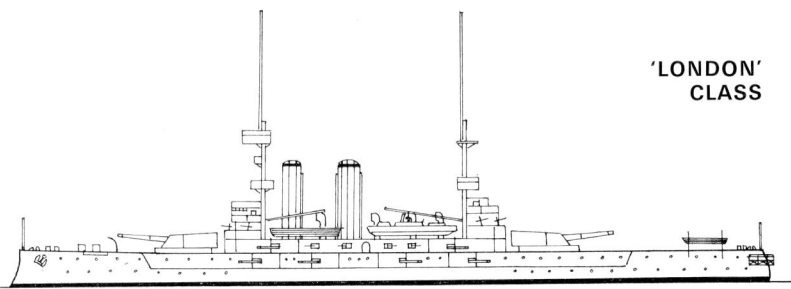

Venerable   MoD   _c.1908_

'LONDON' CLASS

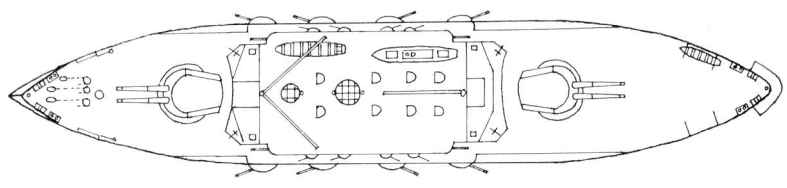

London   MoD   6/1902

Overall dark grey replaced the Victorian black and white colour scheme in 1903.
Funnel bands as an identifying symbol were introduced in 1909, as shown below.

LONDON, 1903

Russell   MoD   *c. 1906*

1901
DUNCAN, RUSSELL, ALBEMARLE, CORNWALLIS, EXMOUTH, MONTAGUE
14,000 tons
429′ OA × 75′
4 × 12 inch, 12 × 6 inch × 12 × 12 pdr, 6 × 3 pdr, 4 × 18 inch TT
Triple Expansion (see text), 18,000 HP, 19 knots
780

THIS class differed externally slightly in having two comparatively large equal-sized funnels. The **London, Formidable** and later **Queen** classes had a thinner fore funnel, and the upper battery of 12 pdr guns were mounted on the open main deck amidships. In machinery this class had four-cylinder Triple Expansion engines, as opposed to three cylinders in earlier classes and the **Queen** class; two low-pressure cylinders gave more even running and the increase in HP raised the speed to 19 knots. Several years before World War 1, in 1906, the **Montague** was wrecked on Lundy Island. Apart from the

Exmouth   MoD   1908

Warspite, 40 years later whilst on tow to the ship breaker's yard, she was the only British battleship to be lost in this manner during this century.

Two more ships of this class were lost by enemy action during World War 1 in the Mediterranean. In 1916 the **Russell** was mined off Malta and the following year the **Cornwallis** was torpedoed by the U32. For the first year of the war the other three ships served with the Grand Fleet on Northern patrol duties and, during this period, the **Exmouth** was detached for coastal bombardment off the Belgian coast. Both the **Exmouth** and **Duncan** went to the Mediterranean in 1915 and the former ship took part in the Dardanelles campaign. The remaining ship, **Albemarle,** went even further North and became Guardship at the Russian port of Archangel. As there was no immediate requirement for these ships all three were placed in reserve during 1917, thus enabling their large complements to be more usefully employed, and were scrapped 1919–20.

**'DUNCAN'
CLASS**

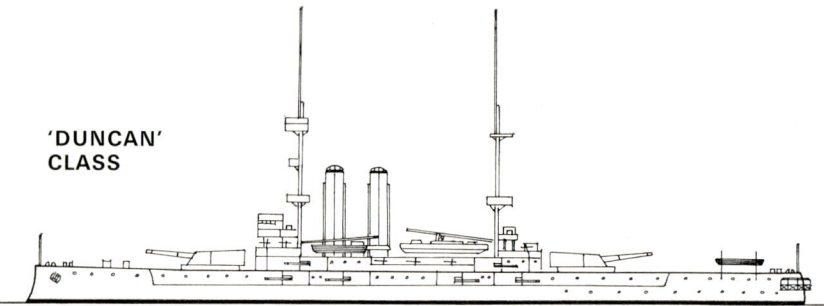

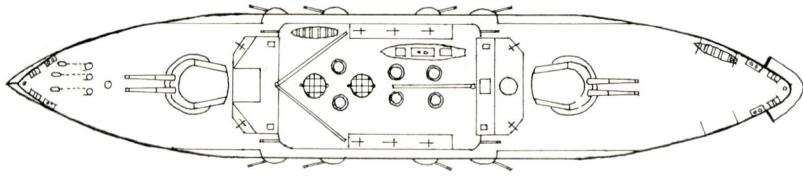

Montague   MoD   c. 1913

Cornwallis   MoD   c. 1912

Prince of Wales   MoD   1906

1902
QUEEN, PRINCE OF WALES
15,000 tons
430' OA × 75'
4 × 12 inch, 12 × 6 inch, 16 × 12 pdr, 6 × 3 pdr, 4 × 18 inch TT
Triple Expansion (see text), 15,000 HP, 18 knots
750

IN many respects these two ships were a compromise between the **London** and **Duncan** classes. Their triple expansion engines, having three cylinders and giving 15,000 HP, were similar to those equipping the **London** class. However, their general layout, except for the thin fore funnel, was similar to the **Duncan** class, which included the 12 pdr guns being mounted in the open on the main deck amidships. At one stage of their careers, before World War 1, both carried two large launches equipped for torpedo firing. These were the last of the pre-Dreadnoughts to mount a secondary armament of 12 × 6 inch guns.

   Both ships saw identical service in World War 1, starting off in the Dardanelles campaign where they were used for coastal bombardment. After this they both formed part of the British squadron of pre-Dreadnoughts, based at Taranto, that helped to blockade the Austrian Fleet. In 1919 both became depot ships for a while before being scrapped in 1919. (It will be noticed that several large ships became depot ships just after the war, for a year or two; this was to absorb the huge numbers of naval personnel awaiting demobilization, as there was insufficient accommodation in barracks.)

Queen   MoD   24/4/1907

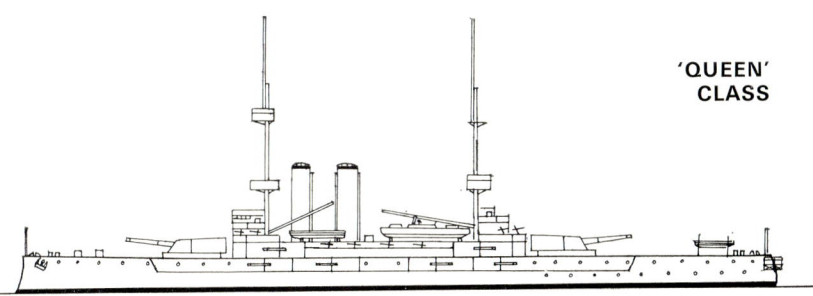

**'QUEEN'
CLASS**

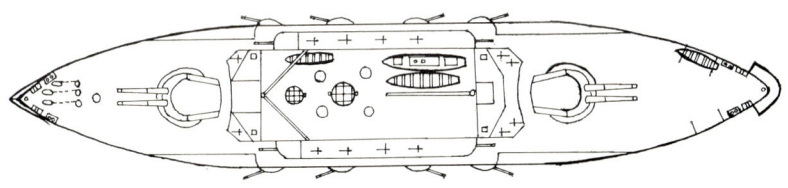

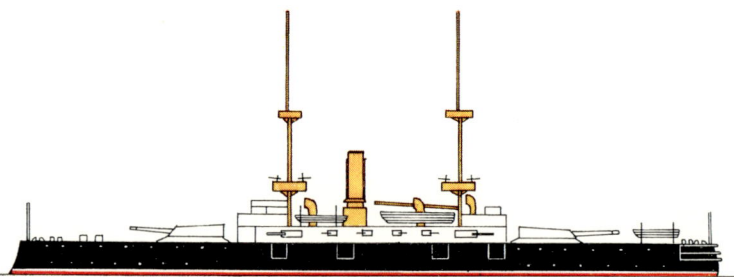

HMS Canopus *in 1906 when a plain grey colour scheme was in use. Note the folded booms for the torpedo nets (T. G. Royall collection).*

The Victorian colour scheme for warships which was used until 1903. A 'Majestic' class battleship is shown. The yellow shade was actually buff-yellow.

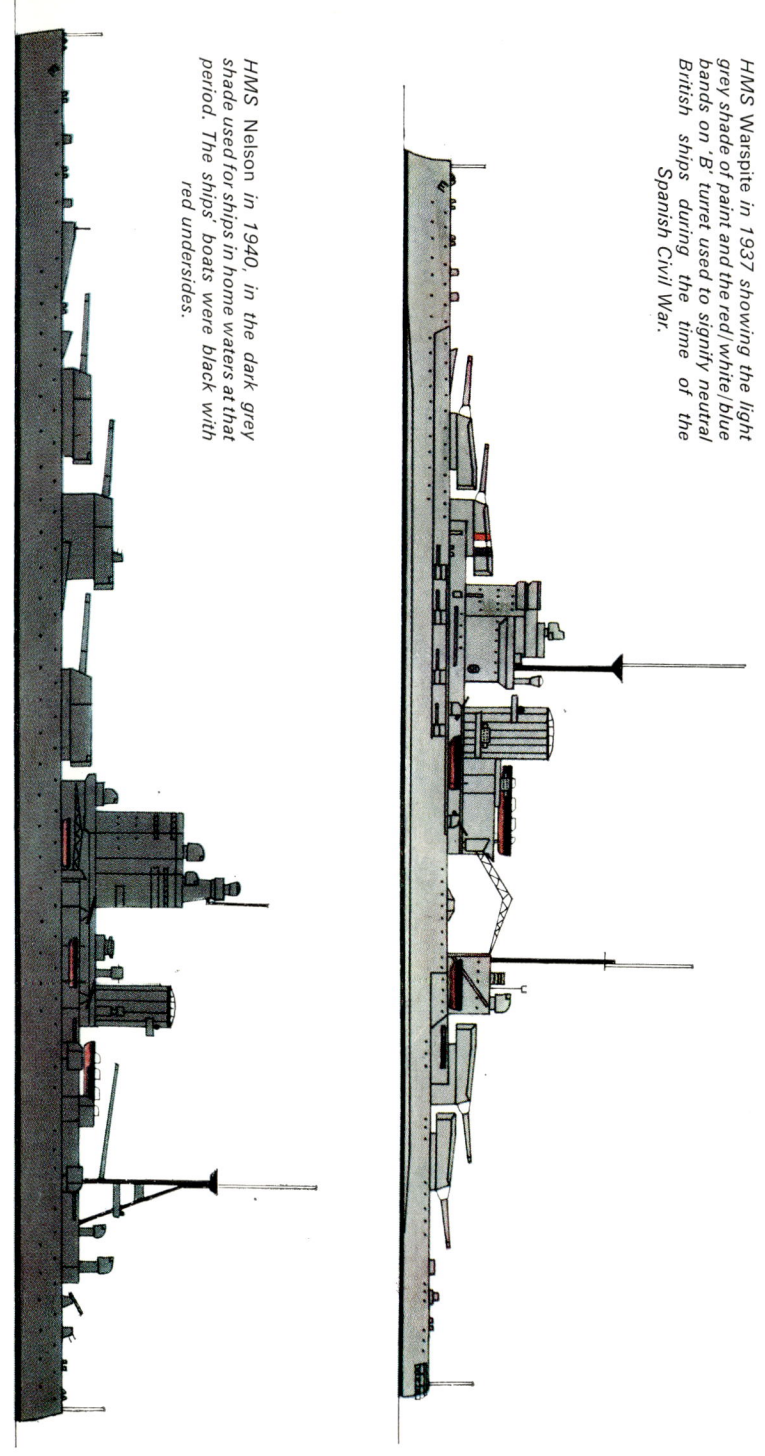

HMS Warspite in 1937 showing the light grey shade of paint and the red/white/blue bands on 'B' turret used to signify neutral British ships during the time of the Spanish Civil War.

HMS Nelson in 1940, in the dark grey shade used for ships in home waters at that period. The ships' boats were black with red undersides.

37

Triumph　　　　　　　　*T. G. Royall*　　　　　　　　1906

1903
SWIFTSURE, TRIUMPH
11,800 tons
470' OA × 71'
4 × 10 inch, 14 × 7·5 inch, 14 × 14 pdr, 4 × 6 pdr, 2 × 18 inch TT
Triple Expansion, 14,000 HP, 20 knots
700

WHILST under construction, for Chile, these two ships were purchased for the Royal Navy and differed in many respects from all the other pre-Dreadnoughts in British service. For their main armament they mounted 10 inch guns, as opposed to the normal 12 inch, and their secondary armament comprised of the much larger 7·5 inch gun. (Although only 1·5 inches larger in diameter this gun fired a 200 pound shell, compared with the 100 pound shell for 6 inch guns.) Foreign navies at this time were using quite heavy guns as an intermediate armament, which led to later British pre-Dreadnoughts having the 9·2 inch (380 pounds shell) armament and eventually the 'all big guns' **Dreadnought.** Being longer and thinner in design these ships were able to make 20 knots speed with their four-cylinder engines. Apart from their length and widely spaced funnels another distinguishing feature, reminiscent of German battleships, were the large goose-neck cranes amidships.

Soon after World War 1 began both ships took part in the Dardanelles campaign and the **Triumph** was torpedoed and sunk by a German submarine. After returning from the Dardanelles the **Swiftsure** was placed in reserve and used as a depot ship. In 1919 she was used as a gunnery target ship before being scrapped a year later.

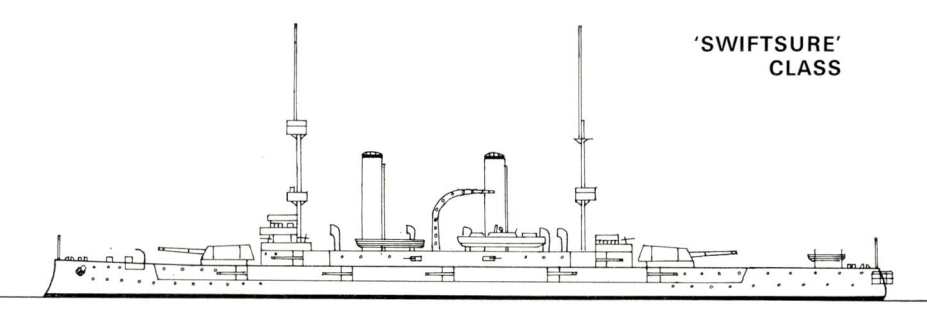

'SWIFTSURE'
CLASS

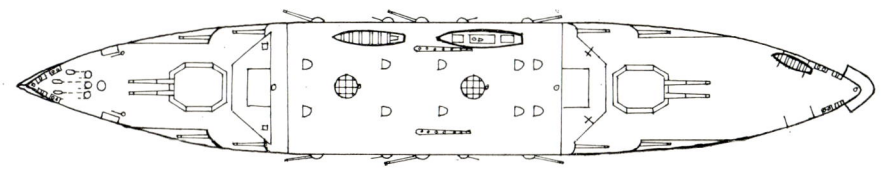

Swiftsure (at Mudros)　　　　　　IWM-Q13822　　　　　　*3/1915*

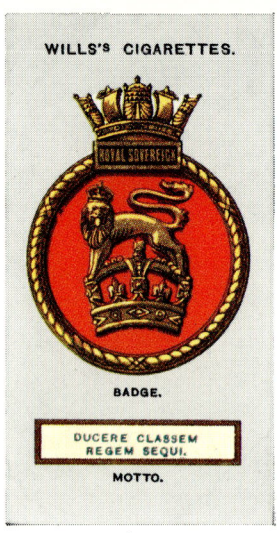

WILLS'S CIGARETTES.

BADGE.

DUCERE CLASSEM REGEM SEQUI.

MOTTO.

WILLS'S CIGARETTES.

BADGE.

ONE IN A HUNDRED.

MOTTO.

These typical examples of battleship badges, all from ships described in this book, are from a set of Wills' cigarette cards issued in the 1930s, 'Ship's Badges in the Royal Navy'. They are reproduced by courtesy of the Imperial Tobacco Company.

WILLS'S CIGARETTES.

BADGE.

FULMEN ERIPIMUS JOVI.

MOTTO.

WILLS'S CIGARETTES.

BADGE.

USQUE AD FINEM.

MOTTO.

WILLS'S CIGARETTES.

BADGE.

SEMPER EADEM.

MOTTO.

WILLS'S CIGARETTES.

BADGE.

INTAMINATIS
FULGET HONORIBUS.

MOTTO.

Vice-Admiral Sir Doveton Sturdee on board his Flagship Hercules *in 1915. The ship's unofficial badge, a representation of Hercules, is cast on the brass tampions which seal the gun barrels. In the background the officer-of-the-watch directs sideboys who are securing a lighter or boat alongside.*

Britannia MoD *10/1906*

1905-06
KING EDWARD, COMMONWEALTH, DOMINION, HINDUSTAN, ZEALANDIA (Ex-New Zealand), HIBERNIA, AFRICA, BRITANNIA

16,350 tons
454′ OA × 78′
4 × 12 inch, 4 × 9·2 inch, 10 × 6 inch, 12 × 12 pdr, 14 × 3 pdr, 4 × 18 inch TT
Triple Expansion (4 cylinders), 18,000 HP, 19 knots
777

AS a result of several foreign navies increasing the intermediate armament of their battleships, 4 × 9·2 inch guns were included in the armament of this class. However, this was not a popular idea in the Royal Navy for, in practice, it was difficult to spot the fall of shot when firing with a mixed main armament. The 3 pdr guns were a new type, being semi-automatic, and fitted on top of the gun turrets. During 1911–12 three ships—**Africa, Hibernia** and **London**—

Hibernia MoD 1908

were fitted with sloping seaplane runways from the bridge to the bows; the first aircraft take-off from a British warship was carried out from the **Hibernia.** This, however, was only for a temporary period as it was realized, from the experience gained, that a special ship would be required to handle aircraft, which led to the seaplane carrier and eventually the aircraft carrier.

When World War 1 began these ships formed a complete Battle Squadron, Number 3, of the Grand Fleet and were irreverently known as the 'Wobbly Eight' due to their age, low speed and lack of armament. By early 1915 they had been withdrawn from the main Battle Fleet and based on the Thames estuary as a counter measure to German battle cruiser raids on the East coast. Soon after this they were dispersed as a squadron and carried out secondary roles.

Two ships of this class became war casualties, the **King Edward** was sunk

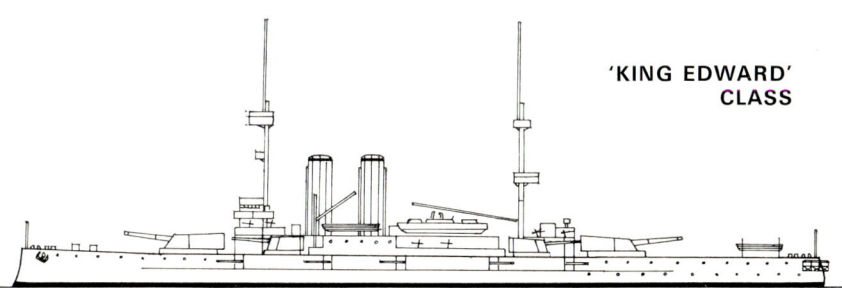

'KING EDWARD' CLASS

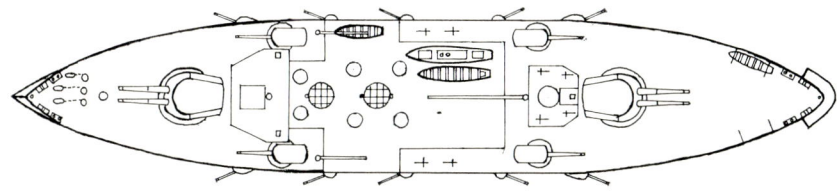

Commonwealth   MoD   1906

by a mine off Cape Wrath in 1916, and in 1918 the **Britannia** was torpedoed by the U50 off Cape Trafalgar. One ship, the **Hibernia,** took part in the Dardanelles campaign and served after this in the Mediterranean where she was joined by the **Zealandia.** Both ships became depot ships before being scrapped in 1921, which was the fate of the rest of the class except **Commonwealth,** which was used as a gunnery training ship from 1918 until scrapped in 1921.

Lieutenant C. R. Samson, pioneer naval aviator, flew this Short S.27 from a flying-off deck built aboard Africa *in January 1912.* Africa, Hibernia, *and* London *all had flying-off decks built over the forecastle and were the first fleet ships to operate aircraft (IWM-Q67863).*

Lord Nelson   MoD   *1910*

1907-08
LORD NELSON, AGAMEMNON
16,500 tons
445′ OA × 79′
4 × 12 inch, 10 × 9·2 inch, 15 × 12 pdr, 16 × 3 pdr, 5 × 18 inch TT
Triple Expansion (4 cylinders), 16,750 HP, 18½ knots
885

THESE two ships were the last of the pre-Dreadnoughts although, due to their advanced stage of construction, they actually joined the Fleet after the **Dreadnought** had entered service. With their large intermediate armament of 9·2 inch guns, as a reply to foreign contemporaries, they were sometimes referred to as 'semi-Dreadnoughts'. In design they were vastly different to all earlier ships with their large 'citadel' superstructure amidships.

Their war service was similar, and started off as part of the Channel Squadron. From there both ships went to the Mediterranean and took part in the Dardanelles campaign and, after this, continued to serve in the Mediterranean for the rest of the war. The **Lord Nelson** was scrapped in 1920, but her sister ship got a new lease of life as the Royal Navy's first radio-controlled target ship. As such she served until 1927, when she was scrapped, being the last of the British pre-Dreadnoughts to go. (Germany, after the severe limitations imposed by the Washington Naval Treaty, retained several pre-Dreadnoughts and two of them—**Schlesien** and **Schleswig Holstein**—saw service in World War 2.)

45

Agamemnon   MoD   *1908*

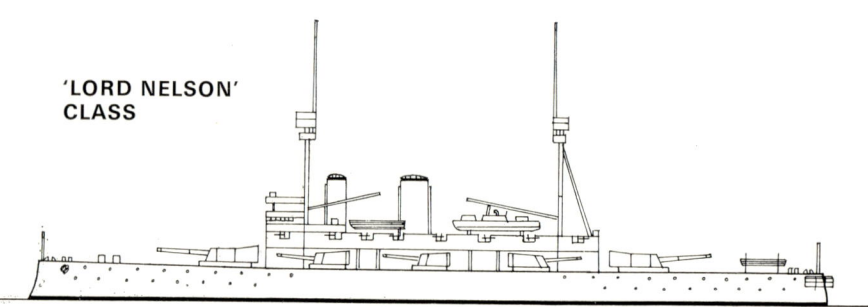

'LORD NELSON'
CLASS

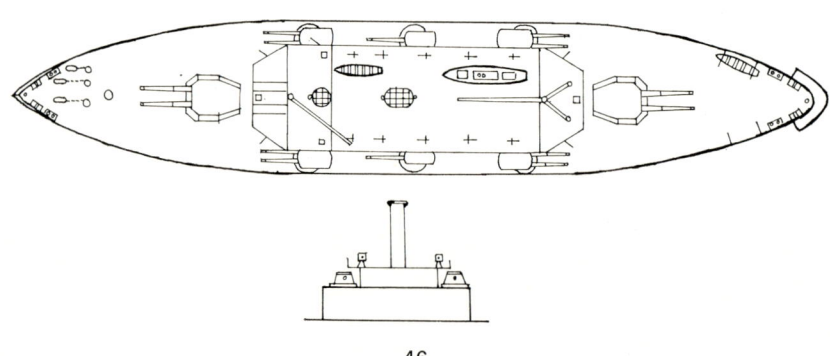

Dreadnought　　　　　　　　　MoD　　　　　　　　　1/1907

1906
DREADNOUGHT
17,900 tons
526' OA × 82'
10 × 12 inch, 24 × 12 pdr, 5 × 18 inch TT
Turbines, 23,000 HP, 22 knots
800

WITH an increasing intermediate armament on pre-Dreadnoughts the next logical step in the construction of battleships was to increase the main armament and dispense with the intermediate. This would mean increasing the number of 12 inch gun turrets to four or more to make it a worthwhile proposition and, to put even more urgency into the project, the USA already had plans for such ships. In October 1905 the **Dreadnought** was laid down, and launched only a few months later in February 1906; she was ready for trials in October 1906, being the only British battleship ever to be constructed in one year.

There was no doubt that her arrival startled the maritime powers of the world for here was the battleship, with 10 × 12 inch guns, that made all contemporaries obsolete at once. Steam turbines had been used for the first time, raising the battleship's speed to 22 knots, and the old reciprocating triple expansion engines in earlier ships could never be modified to increase their speed to this figure. Furthermore, four screws were mounted, as opposed to two in pre-Dreadnoughts, and were to remain standard for all later large British warships. Only a light secondary armament was carried in the form of 24 × 12 pdr guns. (The 12 pdr gun was 3 inches in diameter.) Other navies started at once to build their own versions of the **Dreadnought,** but it was not until 1909 that they were ready. Two examples were the American **South Carolina** with

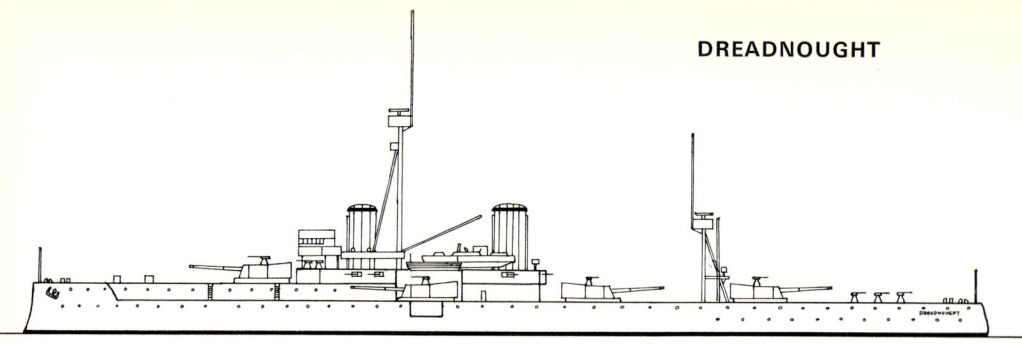

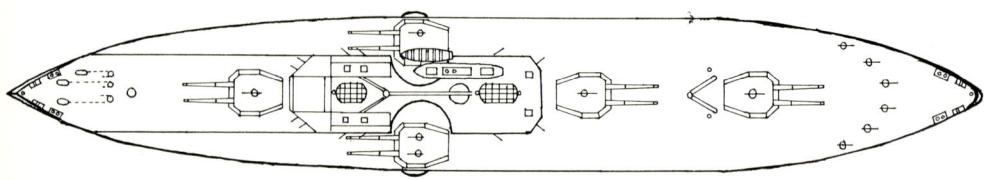

8×12 inch guns and a broadside of all guns, and the German **Westfalen** with 12×11 inch guns and a broadside of only eight due to turret arrangement.

When World War 1 commenced **Dreadnought** led the 4th BS (Battle Squadron) and in 1915 sunk the U29. (This submarine had sunk the cruisers **Aboukir, Cressy** and **Hogue** just after war started.) Under refit, at the time of the Battle of Jutland, the **Dreadnought** saw little more active service and was placed in reserve during 1919. Three years later she was scrapped.

Dreadnought   *T. G. Royall*   *9/1907*

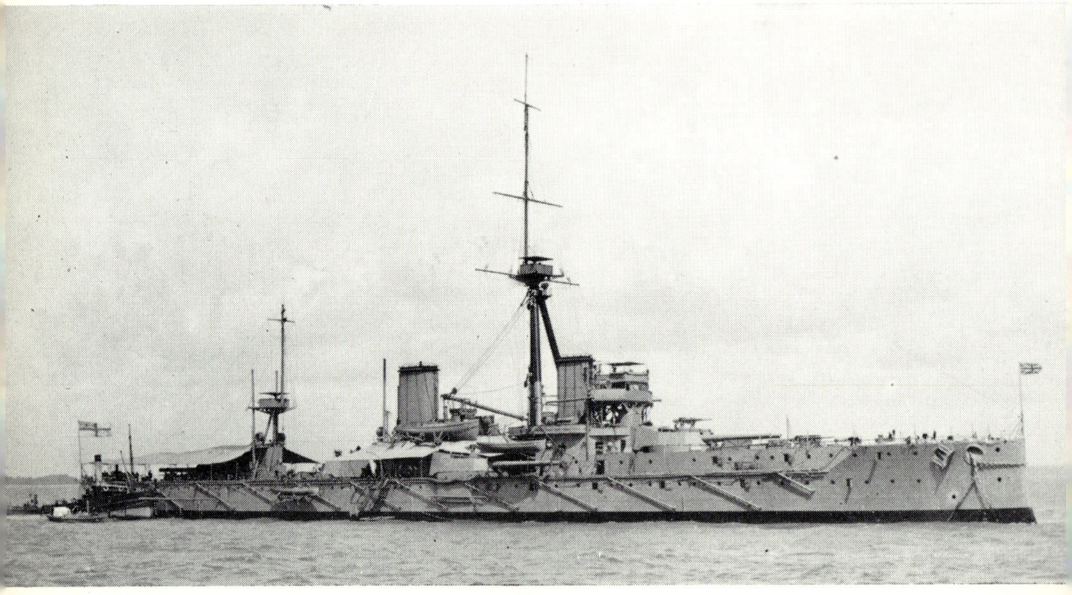

Bellerophon   *MoD*   *1910*

1909
TEMERAIRE, BELLEROPHON, SUPERB
18,600 tons
526' OA × 82'
10 × 12 inch, 16 × 4 inch, 3 × 18 inch TT
Turbines, 23,000 HP, 22 knots
850

LAID down shortly after the **Dreadnought** had entered service these three ships were completed two years later. As was to be expected they were very similar to the earlier ship, incorporating the same machinery and with identical dimensions. An increased secondary armament was mounted, 4 inch guns as opposed to 12 pdr, which it was realized were too small to deal with torpedo craft (a 4 inch shell weighed 25 pounds). Also a tripod mainmast was installed with a gunnery spotting top.

All three ships took part in the Battle of Jutland and served with the Grand Fleet in home waters for most of World War 1. In 1918 the **Temeraire** and **Superb** went to the Mediterranean and there the latter ship led the Allied Fleet through the Dardanelles when Turkey surrendered. The **Bellerophon** and **Superb** became gunnery training ships in 1919 and, at the same time, the **Temeraire** became a cadets' training ship. After two years in these roles all were scrapped during 1921–22.

Temeraire   MoD   14/7/1909

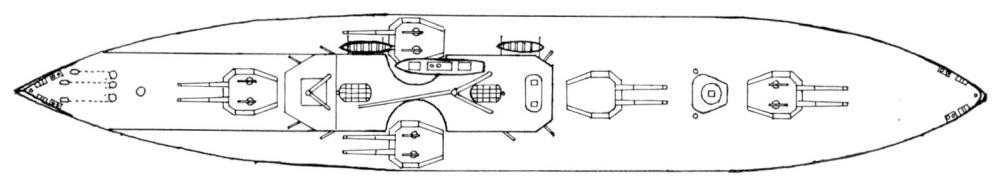

'TEMERAIRE'
CLASS

Superb   MoD   1909

1910
ST. VINCENT, COLLINGWOOD, VANGUARD

19 250 tons
536' OA × 84'
10 × 12 inch, 18 × 4 inch, 3 × 18 inch TT
Turbines, 24,500 HP, 22 knots
870

THESE three ships were enlarged versions of the **Temeraire** class in most respects. There was an increase in dimensions, displacement and more powerful machinery was installed to maintain a top speed of 22 knots. (This was now considered the minimum top speed for a battleship and, to their constructor's credit, most ships could always manage to achieve more in service.) An improved type of 12 inch gun was mounted, of 50 calibres and therefore longer than earlier marks, and two more 4 inch guns carried. In appearance they differed from the **Temeraire** class, apart from a longer hull and main guns, by having a thin fore funnel.

Their World War 1 service was similar, starting with being part of the 1st BS and all taking part in the Battle of Jutland. In 1917 the **Vanguard** was destroyed by an internal explosion, not due to enemy action, with great loss of life. The other two ships became gunnery training ships in 1919 and were scrapped in 1922.

Collingwood   *MoD*   *1910*

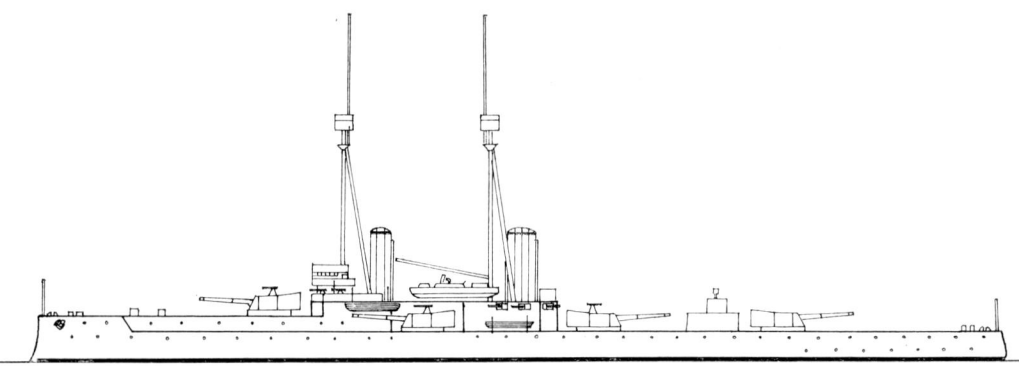

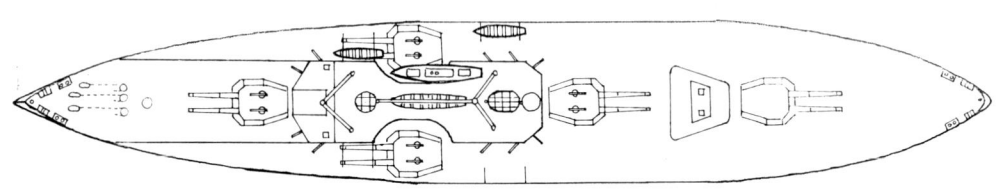

'ST. VINCENT' CLASS

Neptune　　　　　　　　*MoD*　　　　　　　*4/1911*

1911

NEPTUNE
19,900 tons
546' OA × 85'
10 × 12 inch, 16 × 4 inch, 3 × 21 inch TT
Turbines, 25,000 HP, 22 knots
900

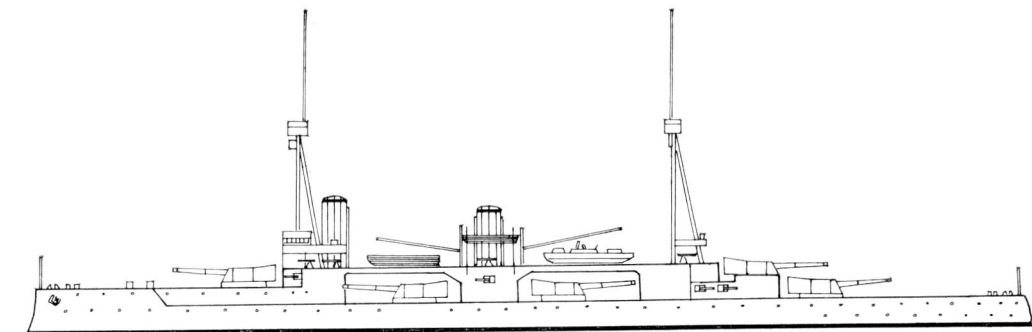

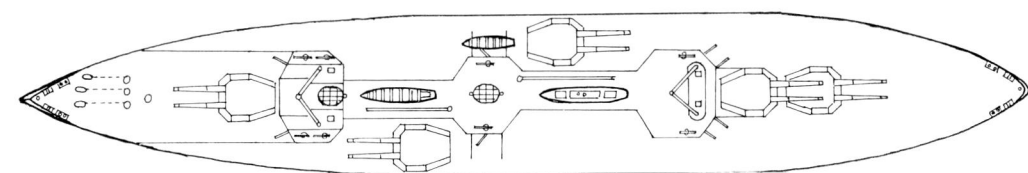

TO make full use of all the main armament for a broadside it was decided to
stagger the wing turrets; earlier ships had them mounted abeam of each other.
They could now train on the opposite side under 'flying' decks. 'X' and 'Y'

turrets, the aft turrets, were superimposed for the first time in any battleship. Instead of open shield guns, often placed on the top of main gun turrets, the secondary armament was incorporated into the superstructure giving more protection to the guns' crews. Slightly more powerful machinery was installed to keep the top speed at 22 knots.

At the start of World War 1 the **Neptune** was serving with the 1st BS, based on Scapa Flow. (Scapa Flow had been selected, before the war, as the Grand Fleet's main base.) She was present at the Battle of Jutland in 1916, and continued to serve with the Grand Fleet throughout the war. Wartime changes included, like most battleships, the addition of anti-aircraft guns, in this case 2 × 3 inch; the forward part of the 'flying' deck was removed and a funnel cap was added to the fore funnel. In 1919 the **Neptune** was placed in reserve and was scrapped in 1922.

1911
COLOSSUS, HERCULES

20,000 tons
546' OA × 86'
10 × 12 inch, 16 × 4 inch, 3 × 21 inch TT (2 × 3 inch AA guns added during war)
Turbines, 25,000 HP, $21\frac{1}{2}$ knots
900

THESE two ships were similar in design to the **Neptune** and had the same main armament disposition and machinery. Absence of a mainmast easily distinguished these ships from the **Neptune,** plus the foremast being mounted behind the fore funnel. During the war the after part of the 'flying' deck was removed and anti-aircraft guns added. With the sole exception of the **Agincourt,** dealt with later in this book, these were the last British battleships to mount 12 inch guns.

Both ships saw similar service in World War 1, starting by being part of the 1st BS. After this both were present at the Battle of Jutland and completed the rest of the war as part of the 4th BS. In 1919 the **Hercules** became headquarters ship to the Allied Naval Commission at Kiel for a while before being scrapped in 1922. The **Colossus** was converted into a training ship and, as such, continued to serve until 1928 when she was scrapped.

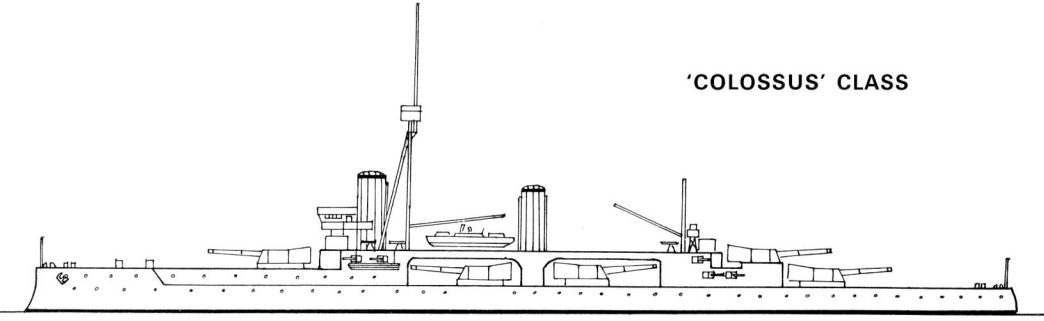

Colossus   MoD   *6/10/1911*

'COLOSSUS' CLASS

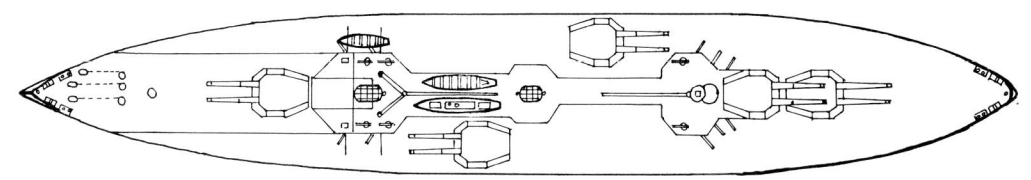

55

Thunderer   MoD   *18/2/1915*

1912
ORION, THUNDERER, MONARCH, CONQUEROR

22,500 tons

584' OA × 85'

10 × 13·5 inch, 16 × 4 inch, 3 × 21 inch TT (3 inch AA guns added during war)

Turbines, 27,000 HP, 21½ knots

900

THIS class introduced the 13·5 inch gun as main armament with the five turrets all mounted on the centre line to give a full broadside. They were sometimes referred to as 'super-Dreadnoughts', on account of having heavier guns, along with later ships, but this title did not become common usage. Once again it is interesting to note how such a small change in gun diameter produced a much heavier shell, 1,250 pounds for 13·5 inch and only 850 pounds for 12 inch. More powerful machinery was installed to give these larger ships a reasonably high top speed of over 21 knots. (A greater percentage of oil fuel, besides coal the primary heat producer, was also used in this class, which was pointing the way to all oil fuel.) For the first time in battleship construction, some measure of protection from gunfire was given to ships' boats amidships.

All had similar World War 1 service, forming part of the 2nd BS throughout the war, and taking part in the Battle of Jutland. Four years after the war, in 1922, the **Orion** and **Conqueror** were the first of this class to be scrapped. Not following the usual fate of surplus battleships the **Monarch** was eventually sunk as a target in 1925. After serving for several years as a cadets' training ship the **Thunderer** was the last to be scrapped in 1926.

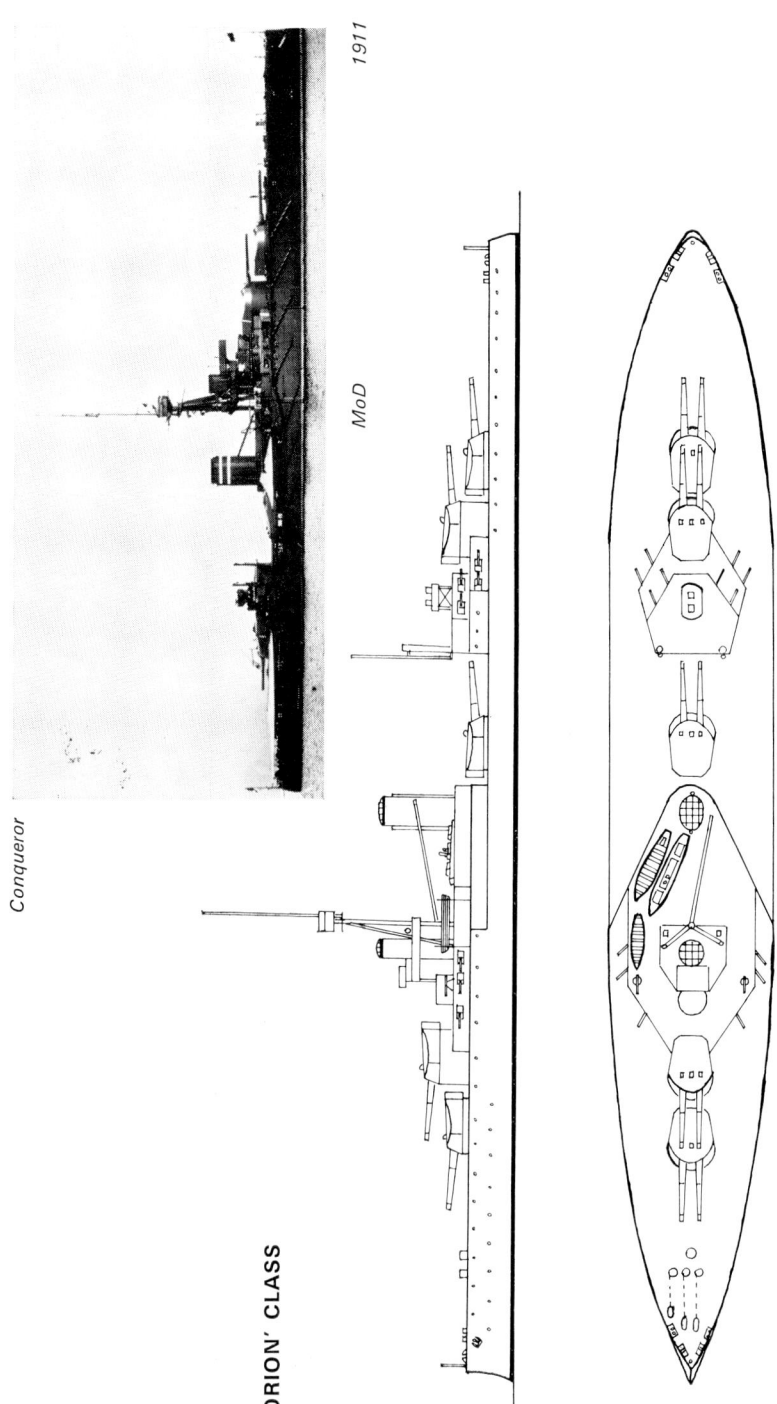

Conqueror

1911

MoD

'ORION' CLASS

57

Centurion   *MoD*   *1914*

1913
KING GEORGE V, CENTURION, AJAX, AUDACIOUS

23,000 tons
596' OA × 89'
10 × 13·5 inch, 16 × 4 inch, 3 × 21 inch TT (AA guns added during war)
Turbines, 31,000 HP, 21½ knots
900

SLIGHTLY larger, but similar in many respects, to the **Orion** class these ships were distinguishable by mounting the foremast in front of the fore funnel. When first completed the foremast was not a tripod and various stiffening supports were tried but, when these failed to impart the desired stiffness to the gunnery director top, the tripod was adopted. The **Centurion** introduced, for the first time in British battleships, director-controlled secondary armament and searchlights which were to prove essential in war. A much heavier shell, of 1,400 pounds, was capable of being fired by the improved 13·5 inch gun which was also mounted in the later **Iron Duke** class. Once again improved machinery was installed to give sufficient power to maintain 21½ knots.

All started their wartime careers in the 2nd BS but, shortly after the war commenced, the **Audacious** was mined. Although badly damaged she was capable of being towed and, during this operation, suffered an internal explosion which sunk her quickly. The other three ships took part in the Battle of Jutland and, in 1919, went to the Mediterranean where the **Ajax** took part in the Black Sea operations. In 1924 the three ships were placed in reserve and two years later the **King George V** and **Ajax** were scrapped.

However, this was not to be the fate of the **Centurion** for, in 1926, she

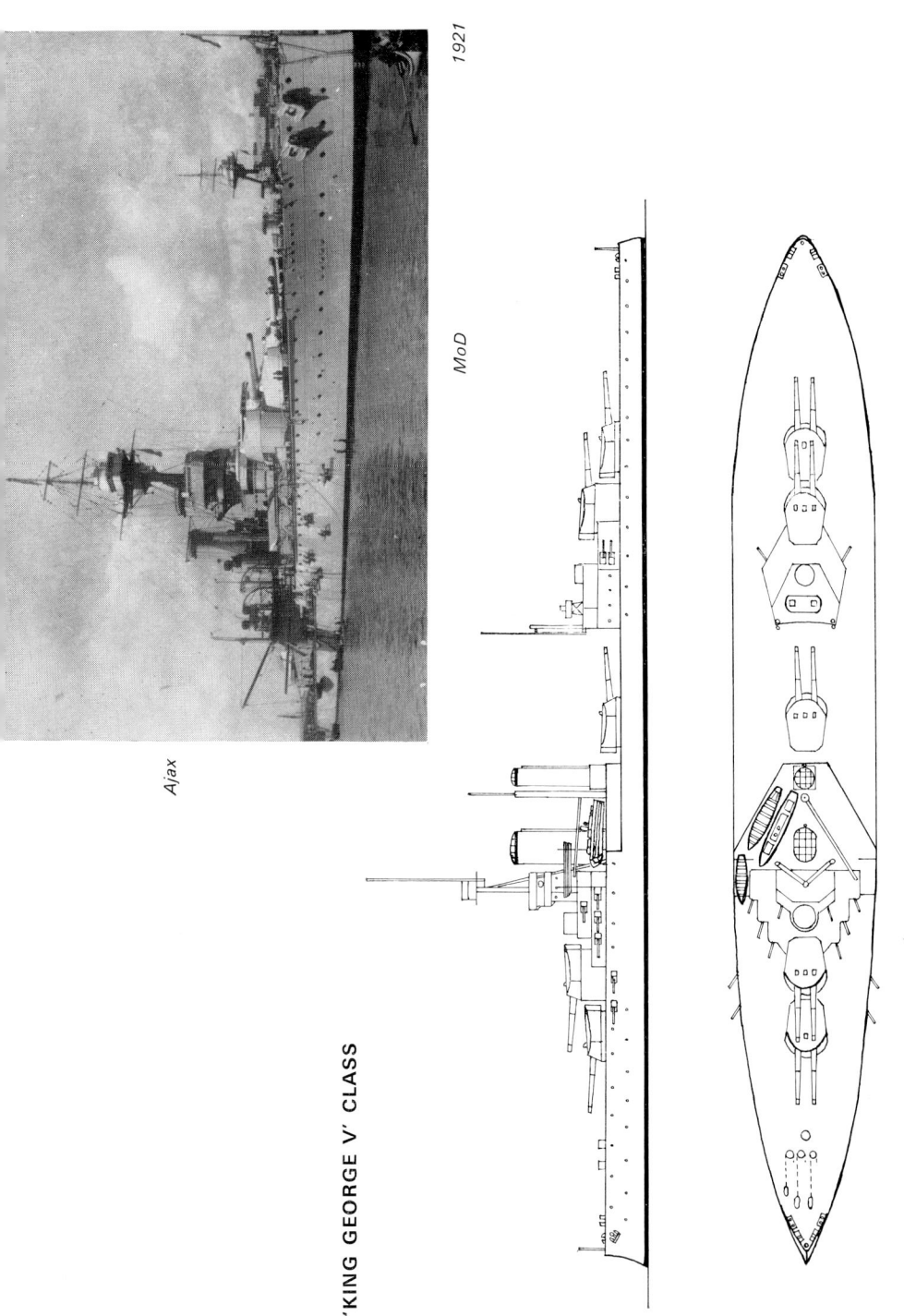

Ajax

1921

MoD

'KING GEORGE V' CLASS

King George V   MoD   3/1913

entered service as a radio-controlled target ship. In this role she was stripped of her armament and non-essential fittings and was controlled by radio, from an attendant destroyer, **Shikari,** being patched up after gunnery practice. As such she gave extremely useful service until World War 2. With dummy gun turrets and superstructure she served as a dummy replica of the new battleship **Anson** and, after this period, she became a floating anti-aircraft battery at Suez in 1942. Finally she became a blockship, forming part of the breakwater of the Mulberry Harbour, in the Normandy landings in 1944.

The battleship Emperor of India *in 1918 carrying flying-off platforms on 'B' and 'Q' turrets on which are ranged Sopwith 1½ Strutters of the RNAS. Several capital ships operated aircraft for 'spotting' purposes in the latter part of World War 1. The 1½ Strutter, a wheeled aircraft, could not be recovered by the ship and returned to land after a sortie (IWM-SP1896).*

Iron Duke   IWM-Q39298   1915

1914
IRON DUKE, BENBOW, EMPEROR OF INDIA, MARLBOROUGH

25,000 tons
620' OA × 89½'
10 × 13·5 inch, 12 × 6 inch, 2 × 3 inch AA, 4 × 21 inch TT
Turbines, 30,000 HP, 21 knots
995

IN this class the secondary armament was increased to 6 inch guns and, for the first time, anti-aircraft guns were fitted during construction. Slightly larger than the **King George V** class they were distinguished from them by the thinner fore funnel and mounting of secondary armament. Oil formed nearly half the total fuel and, during the war, they were fully converted to oil burning operation. Entering service from the beginning of 1914 they were, as a class, completed just before the start of World War 1.

From the start the **Iron Duke** became the Flagship of the Commander-in-Chief, Admiral Jellicoe, and served in this capacity for most of the war. As such

Benbow   MoD   9/11/1914

Iron Duke   MoD   1921

she took part in the Battle of Jutland along with the **Marlborough** which, although badly damaged by a torpedo during the battle, managed to reach port under her own steam. Although missing the Battle of Jutland the other two ships served with the Grand Fleet throughout the war.

After the war the four ships served together in the Mediterranean from 1919 and then with the Atlantic Fleet from 1926. (Before being later termed the Home Fleet there were various names for this force of primarily UK-based warships. Before World War 1 it was called the Channel Fleet; during World War 1 it was the Grand Fleet; immediately after that war it became the Atlantic Fleet and finally—in the early 1930s—it was termed the Home Fleet, the name which became best known.) In 1929 all of this class were withdrawn from first-line service and by 1932 all, except **Iron Duke,** had been scrapped.

Partly disarmed, with two turrets removed, the **Iron Duke** became a training ship in 1933 and continued in this role until World War 2. She then became a depot ship at Scapa Flow, where much of World War 1 had been spent, and served throughout the war. Shortly after this, in 1946, she was scrapped.

Emperor of India   MoD   c. 1920

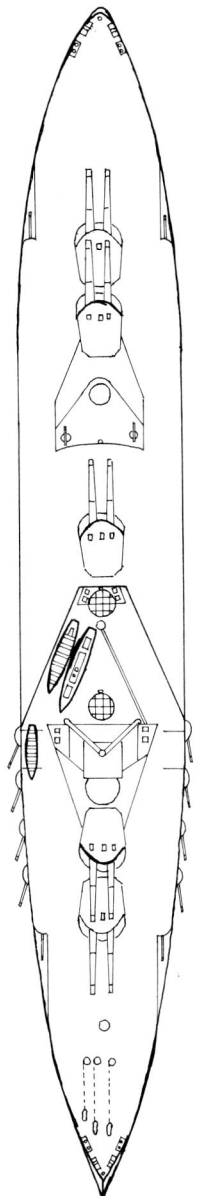

'IRON DUKE'
CLASS

Iron Duke

IWM-SP1459

1918

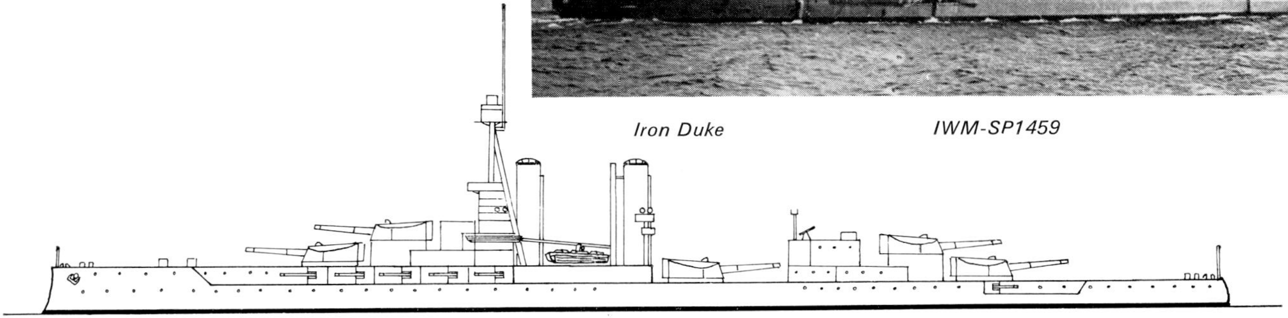

63

Agincourt   MoD   8/1914

1914
AGINCOURT

27,500 tons
652' OA × 90'
14 × 12 inch, 20 × 6 inch, 12 × 3 inch, 3 × 21 inch TT (AA guns added during war)
Turbines, 34,000 HP, 22 knots
1,100

THIS ship and the next two, **Erin** and **Canada,** did not form part of the battle-ship construction plans for the Royal Navy prior to World War 1 as they had been ordered by foreign governments. However, when the war was imminent they were taken over by the British. Originally laid down in 1911 as the **Rio de Janeiro** for Brazil she was to have been armed with 12 × 14 inch guns but, as Brazil already had ships mounting 12 inch guns, this was altered to 14 × 12 inch to simplify ammunition supply. (During this period Argentine, Brazil and Chile were serious rivals for battleship supremacy in South America and came near to crippling their economies in doing so.) When nearly com-pleted, in 1913, Brazil decided that she would not be required and Turkey immediately re-ordered her as the **Sultan Osman 1.** Just before the war commenced she was taken over by the Royal Navy and re-named **Agincourt.**

Her wartime service started with the 4th BS and in 1916, as part of the 1st BS, she took part in the Battle of Jutland. The rest of the war was spent with the Grand Fleet and, being the odd one out, she was discarded and used for experiments from 1919 until 1921 when she was scrapped. Her design was interesting in that she was the only battleship ever in the world to be completed with 14 large guns in seven turrets.

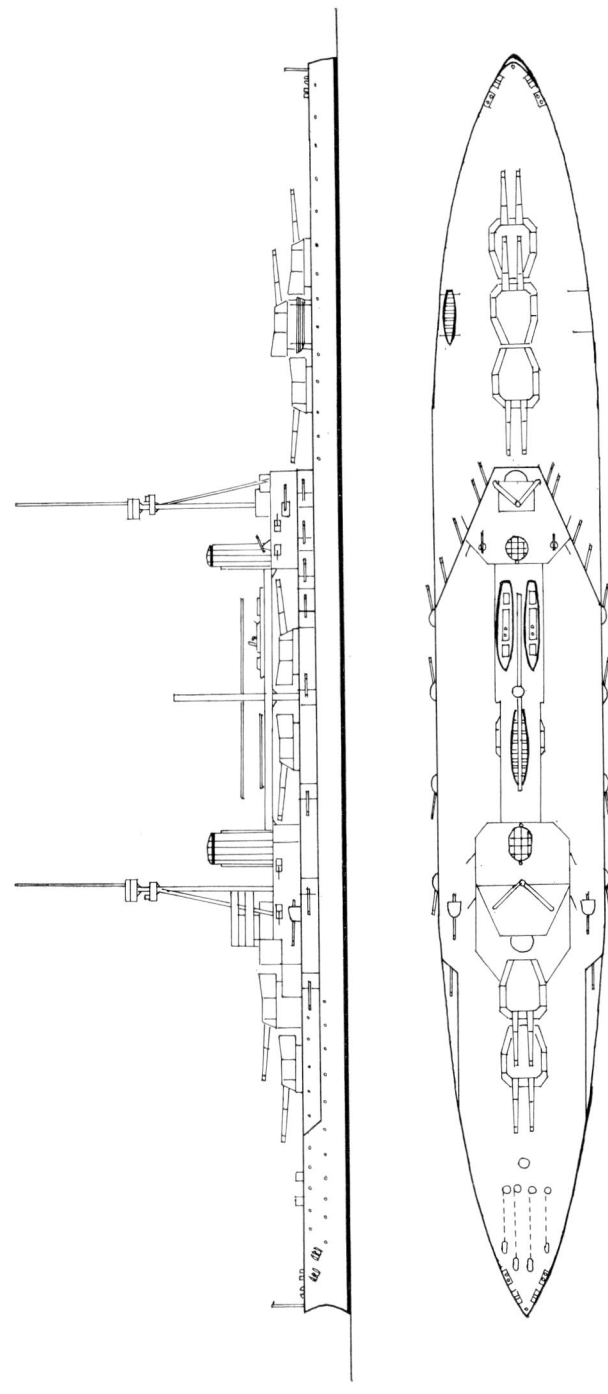

AGINCOURT

Erin   *MoD*   *5/10/1917*

1914

ERIN
23,000 tons
560' OA × 91'
10 × 13·5 inch, 16 × 6 inch, 2 × 3 inch AA, 3 × 21 inch TT
Turbines, 26,500 HP, 21 knots
1,130

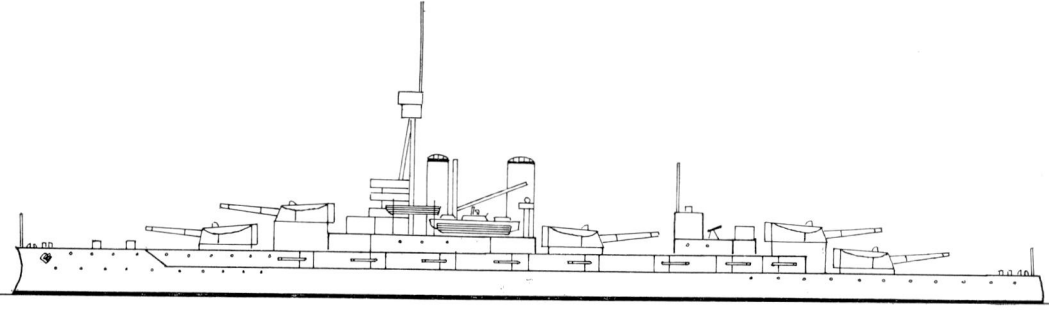

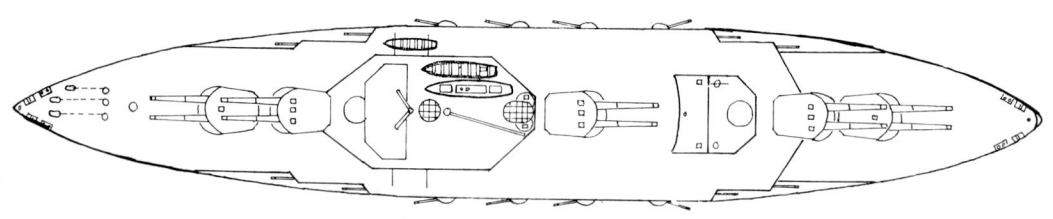

LAID down in 1911 for Turkey as the **Sultan Mehmet Rechad V** this ship was taken over by the Royal Navy, on the eve of World War 1, and re-named **Erin**. Had Turkey taken delivery of this ship and the **Agincourt** the balance of power in the Mediterranean would have been gravely affected. Even if they had never put to sea the presence of these two powerful ships would have tied up several modern British battleships on blockading duties. Thus the Grand Fleet would have been reduced in strength which may well have tempted the German Fleet to take more offensive action than it did. However, fortunately for Britain, these factors were obviously thought of before the war and it was ensured that these ships never left the country. This digression is but a small example of the part battleships played in the world power game at that time.

The **Erin** differed from British ships in having the centre turret, referred to as 'Q' turret, mounted on the upper deck. In 1914 she joined the 2nd BS and served with the Grand Fleet throughout the war taking part in the Battle of Jutland. Placed in reserve during 1919 she was scrapped two years later.

BELOW: In the stokehold of a British battleship. Before the days of oil-firing, coal was the fuel for all powered warships. The task of feeding the furnaces by coal from the ship's bunkers was all done by hand—with shovels (IWM-Q18593).

Canada (stern)　　　　　　　　*MoD*　　　　　　　　*9/9/1916*

1914
CANADA
28,000 tons
661' OA × 92½'
10 × 14 inch, 16 × 6 inch, 2 × 3 inch AA, 4 × 21 inch TT
Turbines, 37,000 HP, 23 knots
1,176

TO hold her position in the South American battleship race Chile ordered, in 1912, two large battleships from Britain to be armed with 14 inch guns; these ships were to be called **Almirante Latorre** and **Almirante Cochrane**. Although not completed when World War 1 started both ships were taken over by the Royal Navy and the **Almirante Latorre** was re-named **Canada**. In appearance she was generally similar to the **Iron Duke** class but armed with 14 inch guns and, being larger, had much more powerful machinery which raised her speed to 23 knots. (Construction was suspended on her sister ship for many years until she was eventually completed, in 1924, as the aircraft carrier **Eagle** which was torpedoed and sunk in 1942.)

The **Canada** joined the 4th BS in 1915 and took part in the Battle of Jutland, the rest of the war was spent with the Grand Fleet. In 1920 she was returned to Chile and reverted to her original name; she served for 40 years in the Chilean Navy before being struck off the active list in 1960.

CANADA

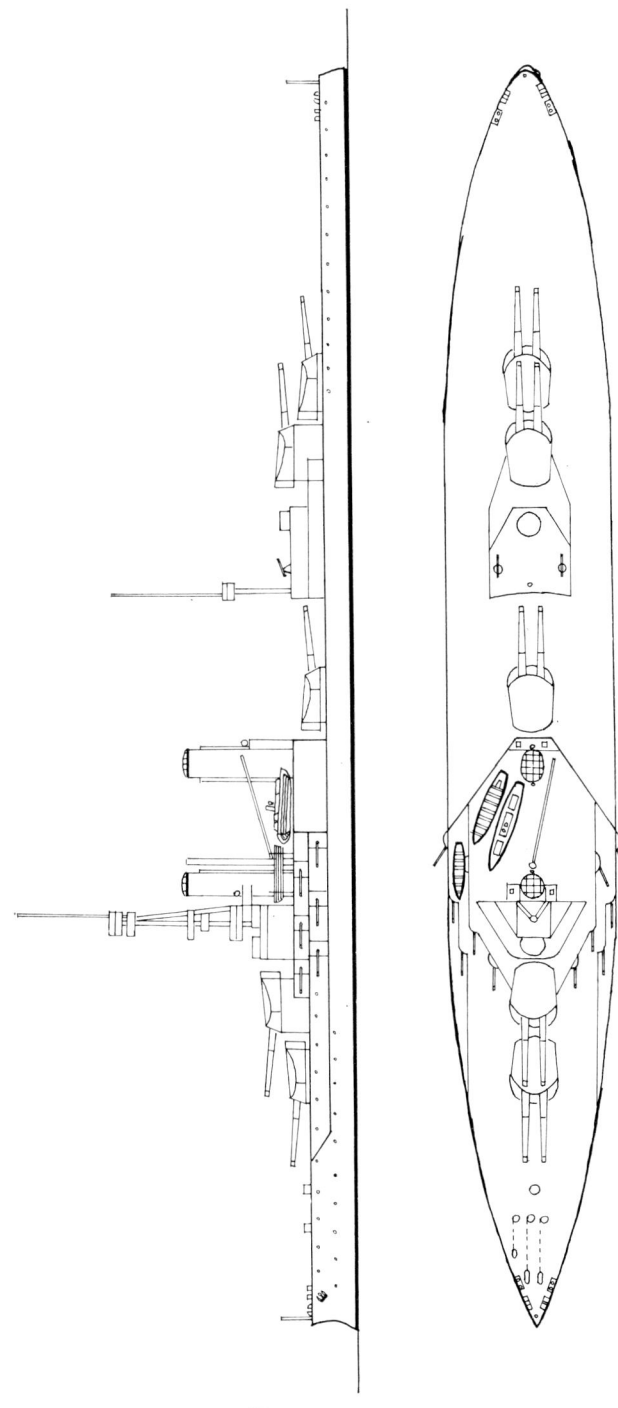

Queen Elizabeth (forward guns)   IWM-Q13238   1918

1915–16
QUEEN ELIZABETH, VALIANT, WARSPITE, MALAYA, BARHAM

As first completed

27,500 tons approx

640′ OA × 90½′

8 × 15 inch, 12 × 6 inch, 2 × 3 inch AA, 4 × 21 inch TT

Turbines, oil fired, 75,000 HP, 25 knots

1,000 approx

THIS class has always ranked amongst the finest battleships ever built in the world and at the time of their completion, during 1915 and early 1916, this was certainly true. They introduced the 15 inch gun to the Royal Navy, all oil-fired boilers and powerful machinery which raised their top speed to 25 knots. With this extra speed they were able to act as links between the battle cruisers—average speed 27 knots—and the battleship squadrons—average speed 21 knots. All were to have been equipped with a secondary armament of 16 × 6

Queen Elizabeth *leaving Mudros harbour in 1915, during the Dardanelles campaign. Note false bow wave painted in white (IWM-Q13817).*

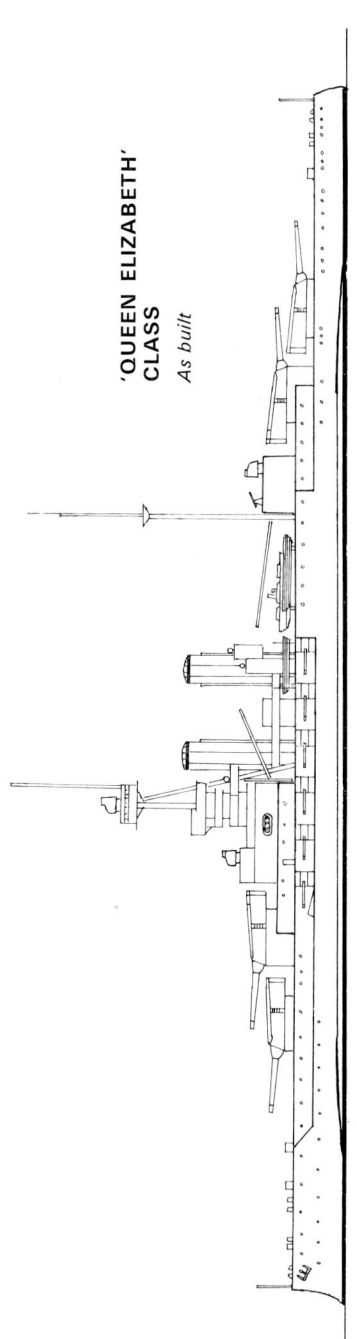

'QUEEN ELIZABETH' CLASS

As built

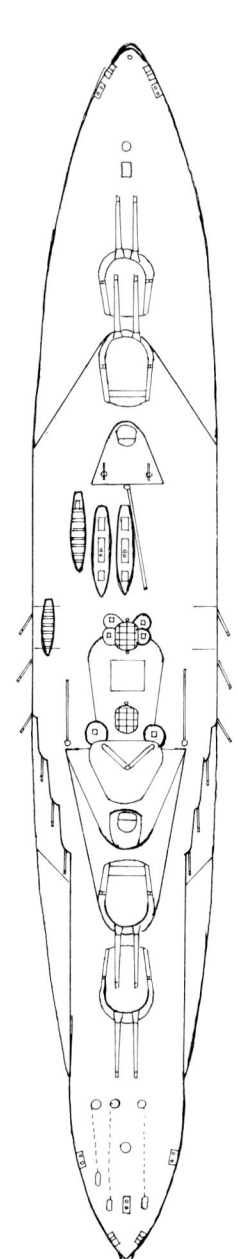

QUEEN ELIZABETH, VALIANT

As modernized and in service,
1939-45

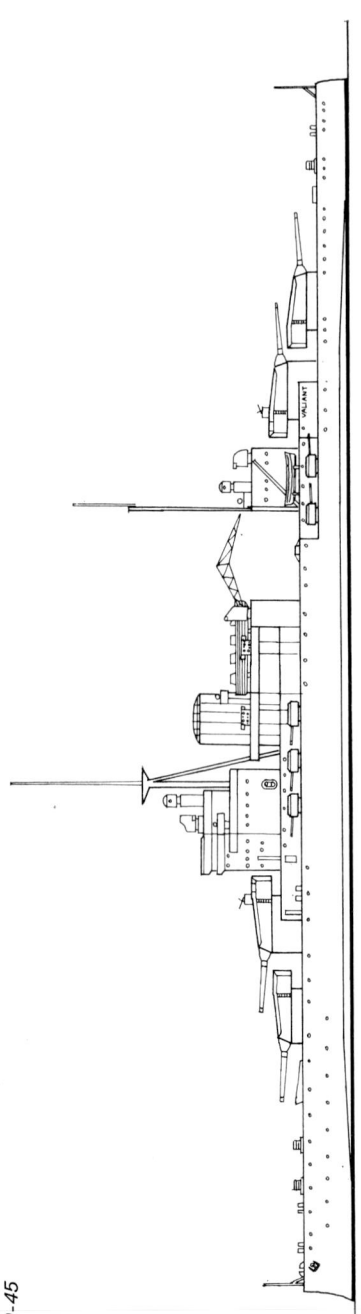
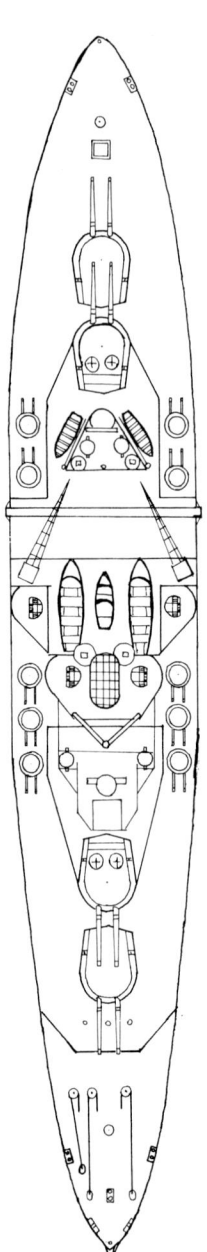

72

Queen Elizabeth   *MoD*   *10/9/1943*

inch guns, four guns mounted aft, but only the **Queen Elizabeth** had these guns which were soon discarded.

Entering service in January 1915 the **Queen Elizabeth,** first of this class to be completed, was sent to the Dardanelles but was quickly withdrawn when several pre-Dreadnoughts were lost through mines and torpedoes. (For actual losses see under the various classes of pre-Dreadnoughts mentioned earlier.) With the exception of the **Queen Elizabeth,** which was under refit at the time, all the rest of the class took part in the Battle of Jutland. They distinguished themselves in this battle by catching up with the battle cruisers, which were suffering heavy damage, and giving them effective support at a critical period.

Valiant   *MoD*   *1932*

Barham　　　　　　　　　　*MoD*　　　　　　　　　　1922

Throughout the war they served together, as the 5th BS, and the **Queen Elizabeth**—the Commander-in-Chief's Flagship—escorted the German Fleet to Scapa Flow when they surrendered.

Between the two world wars they served in the Home and Mediterranean Fleets and were progressively reconstructed which completely altered their original appearance. The first major modification made, in the early 1920s, to all ships was the trunking of the fore funnel into the rear funnel and the addition of anti-torpedo bulges. With the increased beam their displacement was raised to approximately 31,000 tons. Ten years later the **Warspite** was taken in hand for extensive reconstruction and, in 1937, appeared with a modern enclosed bridge, aircraft hangar—which could accommodate four aircraft—and catapult, 8×4 inch AA guns, multiple pom-poms, 8×6 inch guns and strengthened deck armour. Except for retaining her old-fashioned bridge and original 12×6 inch guns the **Malaya** was also reconstructed in a similar manner during the same period. As soon as these two ships had completed their refit the **Queen Elizabeth** and **Valiant** began theirs. When completed they were similar to the **Warspite** but mounted $20 \times 4\cdot5$ inch guns; these were dual purpose, and the 6 inch guns were discarded. As World War 2 had started there was no time to carry out such extensive work on the **Barham**. (See the four different drawings of these ships which illustrate their varying appearances.)

Once again, in World War 2, this class was to give good service. The **Warspite** took part in the second Battle of Narvik, in 1940, and sank several German destroyers and from there went on to the Mediterranean to become Admiral Cunningham's Flagship. There in 1941, with her sister ships **Barham** and **Valiant,** she sank three Italian heavy cruisers at the Battle of Matapan. In 1943 she was present at the Anzio landings, where she was damaged by a

OPPOSITE: HMS Queen Elizabeth, *in superb condition, passes astern of USS* New York *at the Grand Fleet anchorage, Rosyth, in 1918. Note the canvas baffles between the funnels to confuse enemy rangefinders, and the turrets marked off in degrees for gun training purposes. After 6-inch broadside guns can be seen to have been removed (IWM-Q18576).*

Warspite　　　　　　　　　　MoD　　　　　　　　　10/6/1944
(bombarding Normandy)

German flying bomb, and went on to give heavy gun support during the Normandy landings. Eventually in 1947, on her way to the shipbreakers, she was wrecked at Prussia Cove, Cornwall, and broken up there.

As mentioned above the **Barham** took part in the Battle of Matapan and, tragically, was torpedoed by a U-boat shortly after this and blew up with most of her crew. For most of the war the **Queen Elizabeth** and **Valiant** served together and, whilst in the Mediterranean, were severely damaged by Italian frogmen in Alexandria harbour; had they not been anchored in shallow water they would have become total losses. After lengthy repairs had been carried out they finished their war service as part of the British Pacific Fleet. The **Malaya,** whose original cost had been paid for by the Malayan rulers, served in the Mediterranean for a period but was mainly employed on convoy escort duties. After the war, in 1948, all three ships were scrapped.

Malaya (added radar)　　　　　　MoD　　　　　　　　　1944

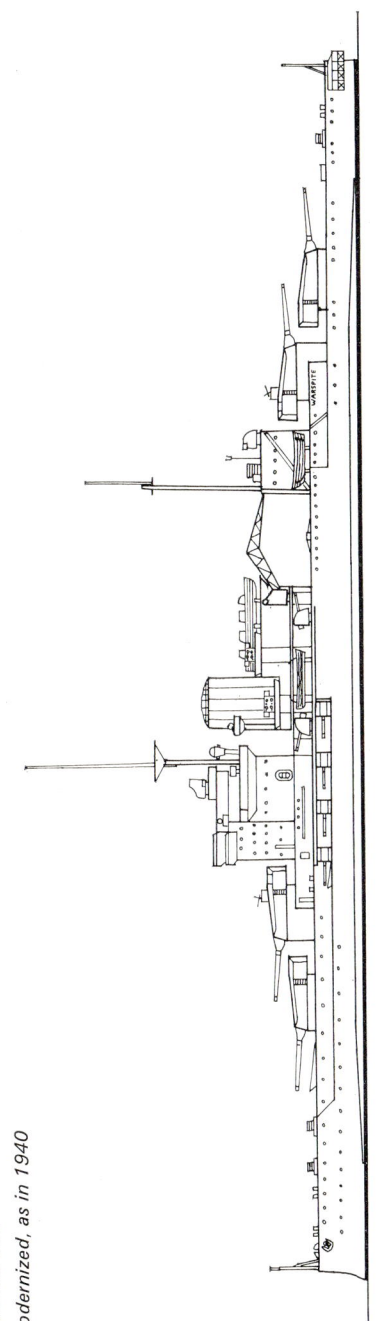
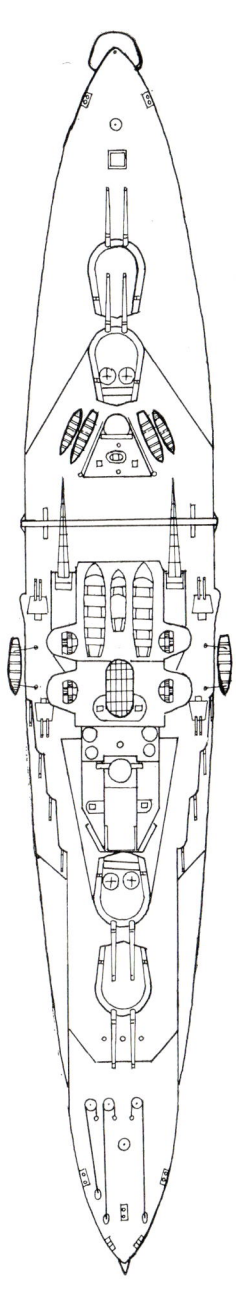

WARSPITE

Modernized, as in 1940

Warspite   MoD   27/3/1943

Queen Elizabeth   MoD   1935

Malaya   MoD   c. 1928

78

MALAYA, BARHAM
After first modernization

Main drawing: Malaya
Inset drawing: Barham

79

Royal Oak   MoD   *1937*

1916–17
ROYAL SOVEREIGN, ROYAL OAK, RAMILLES,
REVENGE, RESOLUTION

27,000 tons (29,190 tons when bulges added)
624' OA × 90' (102' beam when bulges added)
8 × 15 inch, 12 × 6 inch, 2 × 3 inch AA, 4 × 21 inch TT
Reconstructed as above but 8 × 4 inch AA and multiple pom-poms instead of
2 × 3 inch AA, 1 aircraft in **Resolution**
Turbines, 40,000 HP, 21–22 knots
950 approx (1,100 when modernized)

ORIGINALLY there were to have been seven ships in this class but two of them
were re-designed completely and became the battle cruisers **Renown** and
Repulse. Although powerful ships they were never as popular as the **Queen
Elizabeth** class, being slower with their under-powered machinery. When
laid down they were to have been coal-burning ships but the design was
altered so that oil fuel only was used.

Two of this class, the **Revenge** and **Royal Oak,** were completed in time to
take part at the Battle of Jutland where they served as part of the 1st BS. As the
other ships entered service they joined the first two in the 1st BS in which they
served throughout World War 1. (The last ship to join was the **Ramilles**
which was delayed because of damage when she was launched.)

Between the wars they served with Battle Squadrons, normally the whole
class forming one squadron, in the Home and Mediterranean Fleets. Anti-
torpedo bulges were fitted to all ships, which reduced their speed by 1 knot,

80

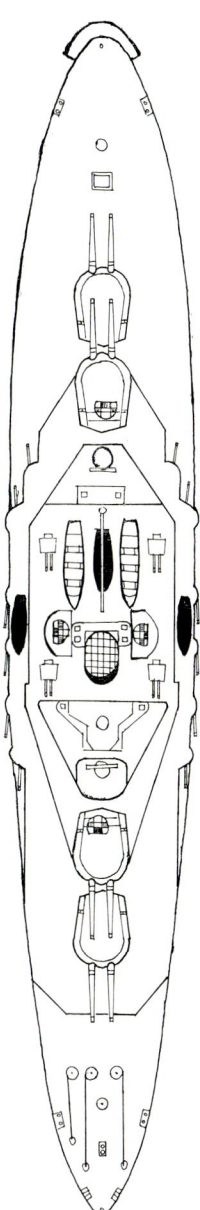

Royal Oak

MoD

1937

Drawing shows Revenge; others lacked Admiral's walk. Resolution had catapult and aircraft on 'X' turret, and Ramilies had tripod main mast. Originally lacked funnel cowl.

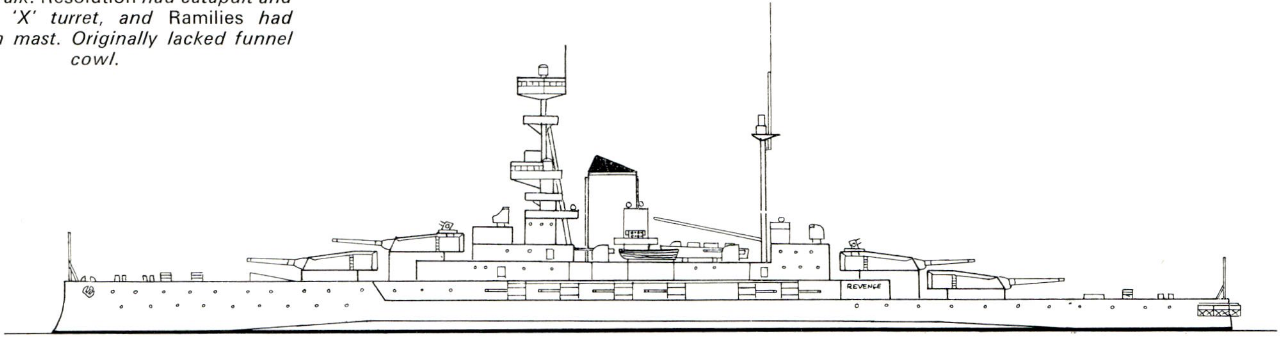

'ROYAL SOVEREIGN' CLASS

Royal Sovereign (added AA and radar)   *14/9/1943*

and additional anti-aircraft guns were fitted. However, because of their dubious value, they were never reconstructed to the same extent as the **Queen Elizabeth** class.

Shortly after World War 2 started the **Royal Oak,** lying in Scapa Flow, was torpedoed and sunk by the U47 in October 1939. Because of their slow speed the remaining ships were used mainly as the heavy escorts for convoys. In 1944 the **Royal Sovereign** was loaned to the USSR and renamed the **Archangelsk;** immediately after her return, in 1949, she was scrapped. The other three ships were all scrapped in 1948.

Resolution   MoD   *28/11/1941*
(Note aircraft on 'X' turret)

Revenge   MoD   *1929*

Nelson   MoD   1945

1927

NELSON, RODNEY

33,900 tons

710' OA × 106'

9 × 16 inch, 12 × 6 inch, 6 × 4·7 inch AA, 3 multiple pom-poms; 2 × 24·5 inch TT, 1 aircraft in **Rodney**

Turbines, 45,000 HP, 23 knots

1,350

IN 1921 plans were made for two 48,000 ton battle cruisers armed with 16 inch guns. However, before construction was started, the Washington Naval Treaty limited the size of capital ships to a maximum of 35,000 tons. As a result of this

Nelson   MoD   4/19/42

Rodney   MoD   *1928*

the **Nelson** and **Rodney** were laid down, in 1922, to a vastly different design and when completed had a most unusual appearance with all their main armament mounted forward. They introduced the 16 inch gun to the Royal Navy; these were the only British ships to mount them although the projected **Lion** class would have done, and a compact style of bridge superstructure which formed the basis of bridges in later ships and the modified **Queen Elizabeth** class. With their high freeboard they proved to be exceptionally good sea boats and were able to maintain their speed in heavy weather.

Before World War 2 both ships served with the Home Fleet and continued to do so throughout the war. Their main use was to provide the heavy escort for many Atlantic and Mediterranean convoys. During the hunt for the German battleship **Bismarck** the **Rodney** was detached from the Atlantic convoy and was able, due to the valiant effort of her engine room crew, to take part in the final action. Both ships were present at the Normandy landings where their large guns gave support in the initial assaults. Three years after the war, in 1948, both ships were scrapped.

BELOW: Rodney (left) and Nelson at Algiers in early 1943 after escorting a troop convoy to harbour. These slow vessels were mainly used for escort work and shore bombardment in World War 2 (IWM-A15990).

NELSON, RODNEY

Drawing shows Nelson.
Rodney had catapult and aircraft on third
turret.

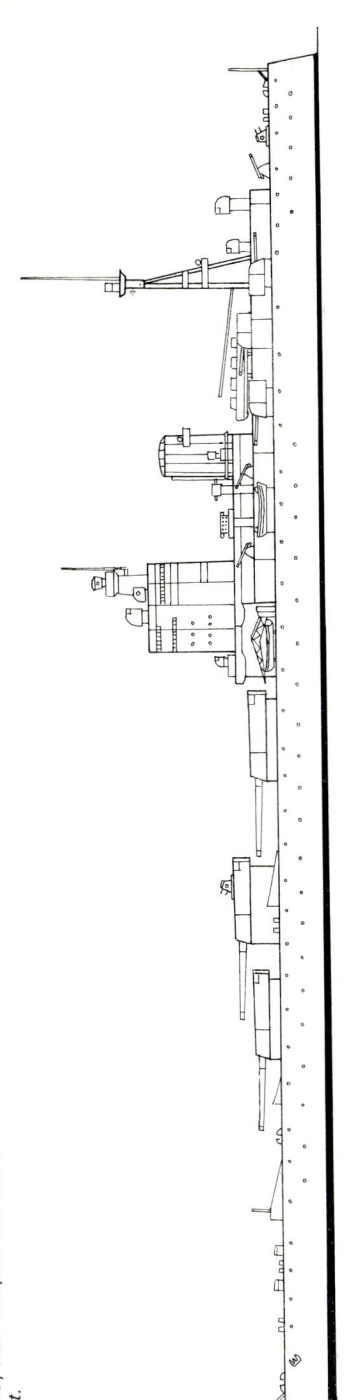
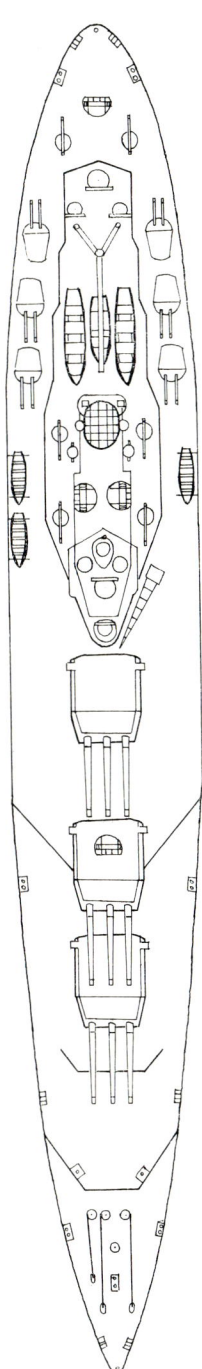

Duke of York (stern)　　　　　MoD　　　　　*28/11/1941*

1940–42
KING GEORGE V, DUKE OF YORK,
PRINCE OF WALES, ANSON, HOWE
35,000 tons
745' OA × 103'
10 × 14 inch, 16 × 5·25 inch dual purpose, 5 multiple pom-poms, 40mm and 20mm added, 3 aircraft
Turbines, 125,000 HP, 30 knots
1,500

THESE ships were ordered under the 1936 and 1937 Naval Estimates and their design was restricted to a displacement of 35,000 tons. A new type of 14 inch gun was introduced which, in practice, was a much better gun all round than the earlier 15 inch. For the combined purpose of secondary and anti-aircraft armaments the dual-purpose 5·25 inch gun was adopted—this type of gun and

86

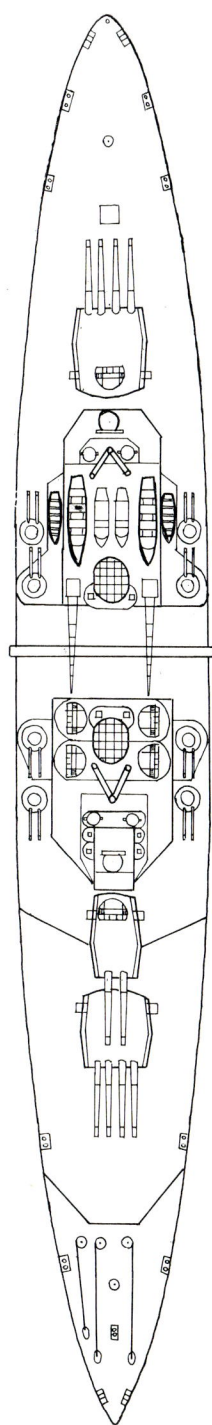

8/5/1941

MoD

Prince of Wales

'KING GEORGE V' CLASS

*As built; extra radar and AA guns added
later.*

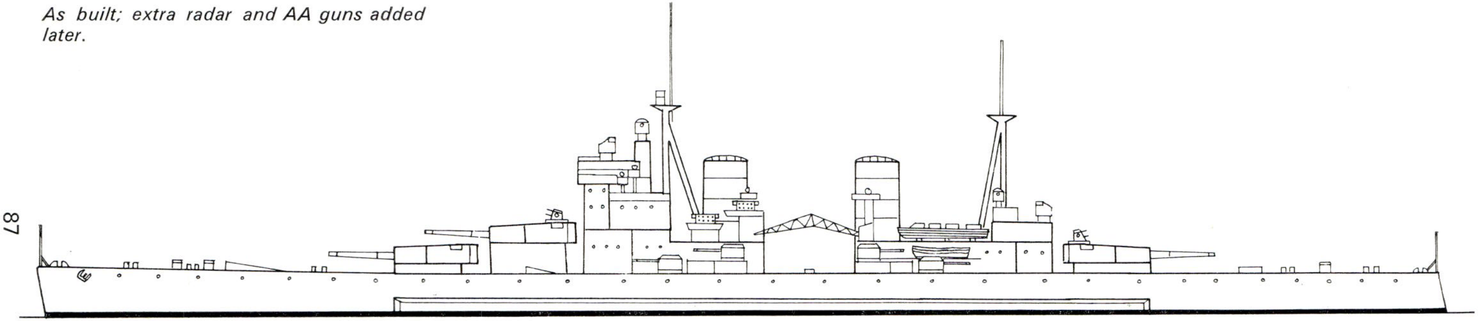

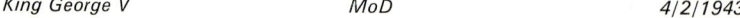

Howe   MoD   10/6/1944

turret was also later used in the light cruisers of the **Dido** classes. Aircraft hangars were fitted on both sides of the fore funnel and a catapult amidships but, as carrier-based naval aircraft became more available later, the aircraft and catapult were removed. With powerful machinery these ships had a high speed and proved to be good sea boats.

During the Second World War this class served all over the world and achieved a good war record. Both the **King George V** and **Prince of Wales** took part in the **Bismarck** action, in 1941, where the **Prince of Wales** was damaged. After being repaired she was sent to the Far East and, with the battle cruiser **Repulse,** was sunk by Japanese aircraft off Malaya. Whilst acting as

King George V   MoD   4/2/1943

88

Anson   MoD   *21/6/1942*

cover for an Arctic convoy, in 1943, the **Duke of York** intercepted and sunk the German battle cruiser **Scharnhorst** in bad weather. As the war in the Pacific mounted all four remaining ships joined the British Pacific Fleet and took part, with the aircraft carriers, in several operations against Japanese held islands.

After the war they were kept mainly in the Reserve Fleet for a long time, in a state of preservation, until future naval policy and requirements were resolved. When the changing pattern emerged it was decided that there could be no further use for these ships and all were scrapped in 1957.

Duke of York   MoD   *1944*

1946

VANGUARD

44,500 tons
814′ OA × 108′
8 × 15 inch, 16 × 5·25 inch dual purpose, 70 × 40mm
Turbines, 130,000 HP, 30 knots
1,600

LAID down in early 1941 her construction became a lower priority when it was realized, from war experience, that the future of the battleship was extremely limited. Four ships of the projected **Lion** class, to be armed with 9 × 16 inch guns, were cancelled but it was decided to carry on with the **Vanguard** as her construction was well advanced. For a main armament it was decided to utilize the 15 inch guns that had been held in reserve, since World War 1, for ships of the **Queen Elizabeth** and **Royal Sovereign** classes. However, although her main armament was old-fashioned, her secondary and anti-aircraft armament was excellent and controlled by sophisticated radar equipment. With the increase in naval air power there was no need to make any provision for scouting aircraft and their associated equipment. Launched in late 1944 she was not ready for service until 1946, after the war had ended.

In 1947 she carried King George VI on the Royal tour of South Africa. Until 1955 she was mainly used as the Flagship of the Home Fleet, but was also utilized in the training role from time to time. Like the **King George V** class her future was limited and, after a few years in the Reserve Fleet, she was scrapped in 1959.

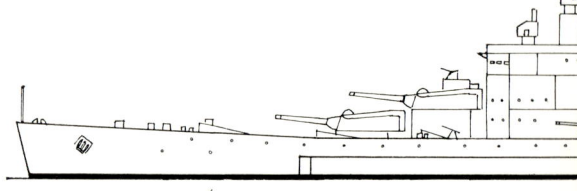

VANGUARD

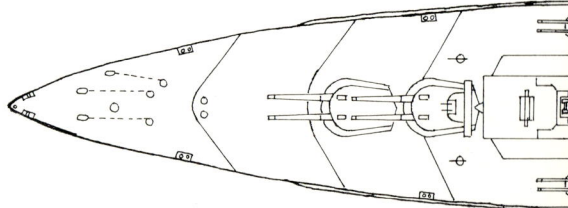

N.B.: Cowls were part of funnel structure, not separate sections.

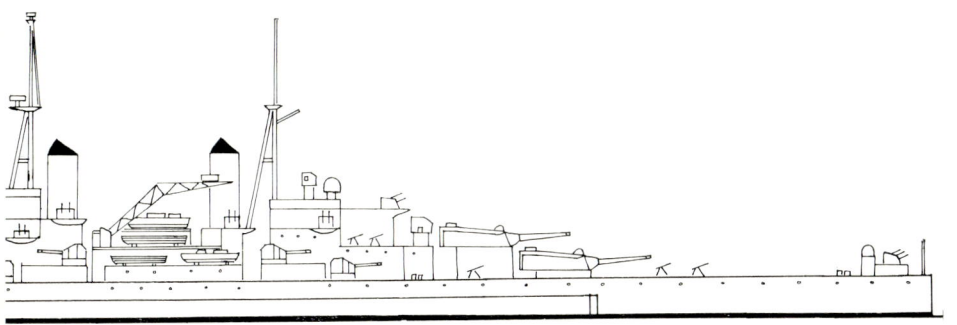

Vanguard   *MoD*   *8/9/1948*

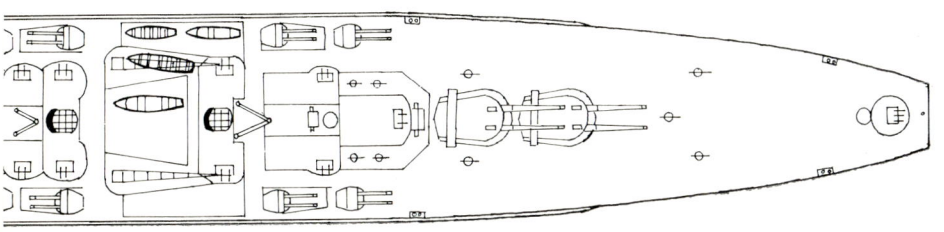

Appendix 1: Funnel Markings, 1909-1914

All colour bands white unless otherwise stated.

MAJESTIC CLASS
All twin funnels

CAESAR

HANNIBAL

ILLUSTRIOUS

JUPITER

MAGNIFICENT (red)

MAJESTIC (red)

MARS (red)

PRINCE GEORGE (black)

VICTORIOUS (black)

CANOPUS

GOLIATH

ALBION

OCEAN

GLORY

VENGEANCE

FORMIDABLE

IRRESISTIBLE

IMPLACABLE

LONDON

BULWARK

VENERABLE (red)

RUSSEL

ALBEMARLE

DUNCAN

CORNWALLIS

EXMOUTH

QUEEN

PRINCE OF WALES

SWIFTSURE

TRIUMPH

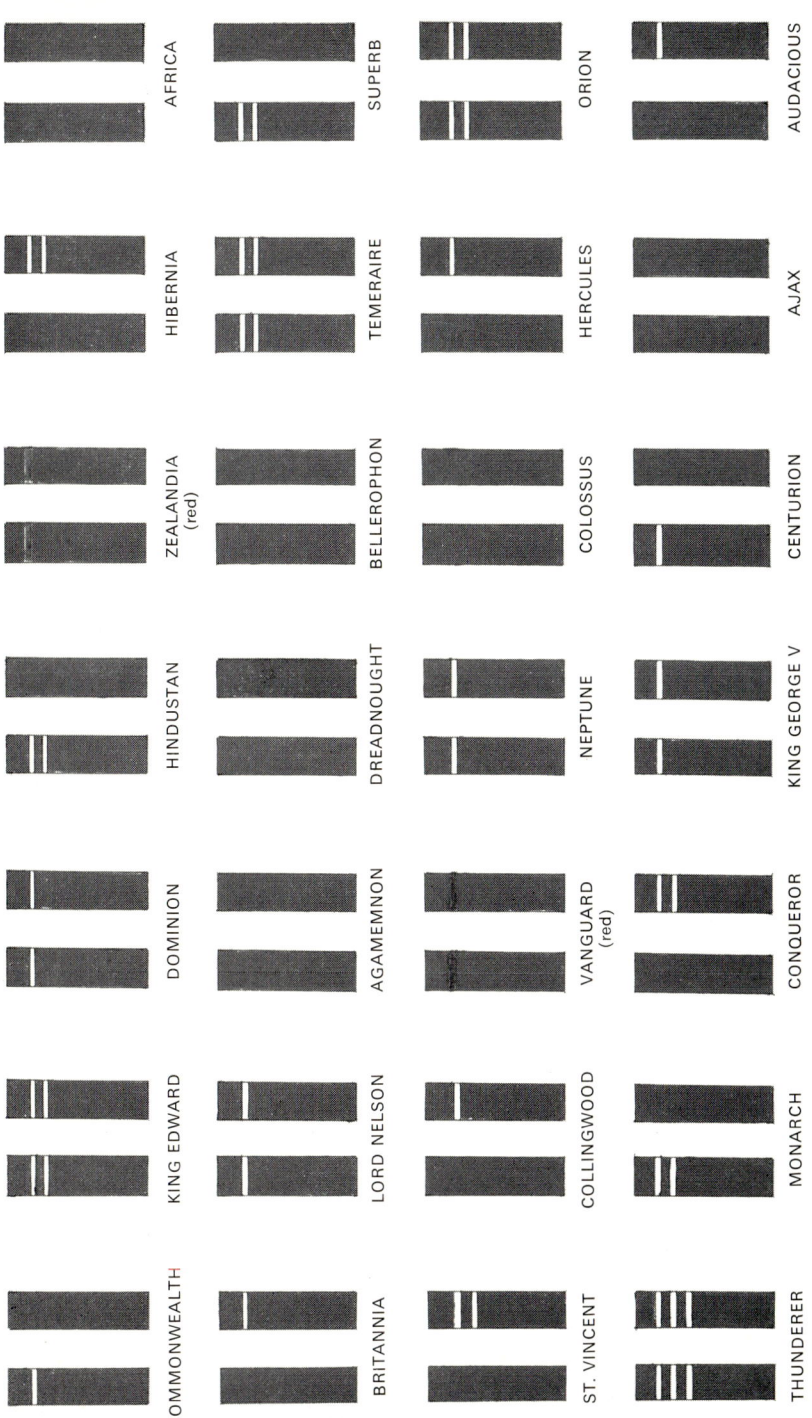

AFRICA

SUPERB

ORION

AUDACIOUS

HIBERNIA

TEMERAIRE

HERCULES

AJAX

ZEALANDIA
(red)

BELLEROPHON

COLOSSUS

CENTURION

HINDUSTAN

DREADNOUGHT

NEPTUNE

KING GEORGE V

DOMINION

AGAMEMNON

VANGUARD
(red)

CONQUEROR

KING EDWARD

LORD NELSON

COLLINGWOOD

MONARCH

COMMONWEALTH

BRITANNIA

ST. VINCENT

THUNDERER

93

Appendix 2: Typical Camouflage Schemes

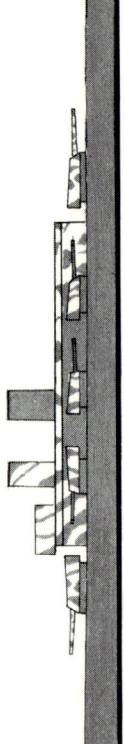

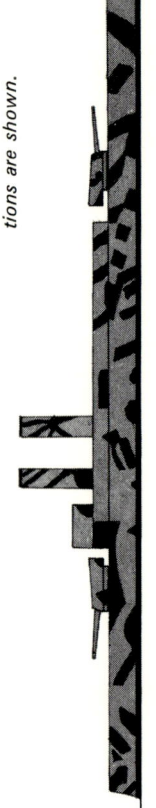

N.B.: Most battleships had plain grey, dark for home waters in the earlier part of World War 1. Some camouflaged exceptions are shown.

Agamemnon in 1915.
Note false bow wave.
White and light grey.

Commonwealth in 1918.
Black dazzle painting introduced in 1917 for some old battleships.

Revenge in 1917-18.
Light grey, dark grey, white, and black.

Indefatigable in 1918.
Dark grey side panel.

Appendix 3: Armament

ABOVE: The complete barbette and quadruple 14 inch gun turret as fitted in a 'King George V' class battleship. The barbette extended to the full depth of the hull as shown in this sectioned scale model. The crew figures give an indication of the huge size of the guns and fittings. The shell handling room and cartridge handling room are in the two bottom levels of the barbette adjacent to the magazines. From here they are taken by hoist to the turret itself.

LEFT: Quadruple 2 pdr Mk VII pom-pom was a widely used close-range AA mounting in most British battleships during World War 2. It was produced in power and hand-operated versions and the shells were tray-fed into each gun which had a rate of fire of 98 rounds per minute from each barrel. Models show the armoured shield round the mounting and the ammunition trays.

ABOVE: Model showing details of the conning position and main gunnery directors on the bridge of a 'King George V' class battleship of the World War 2 period. Main director control tower (DCT) carries a Type 284 surface gunnery radar aerial and the two high angle directors have the 'fishbone' array of the Type 285 radar aerials. In the bridge wings are visual look-out positions for local air defence.

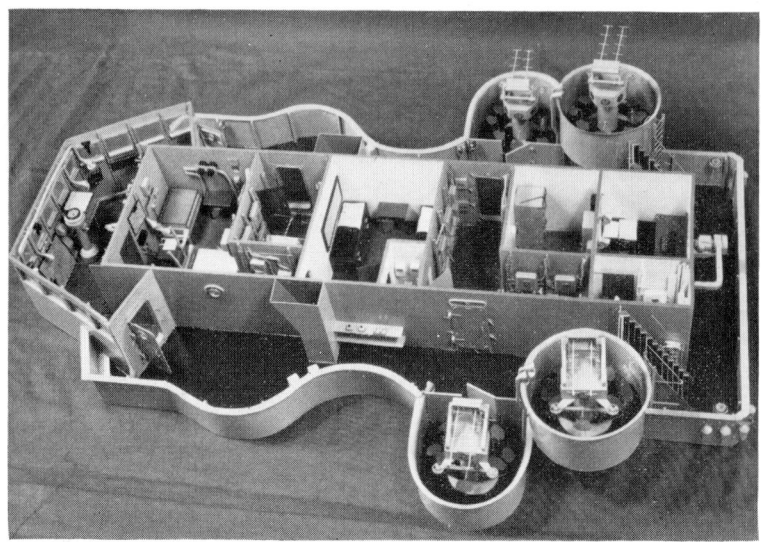

ABOVE: Section through the bridge of a 'King George V' class battleship showing the armoured compass platform (left) with the navigator's chartroom, and the captain's and navigator's sea cabins aft of the compass platform. In the wings are barrage (pom-pom) directors with the distinctive antennae of the Type 282 gunnery radar sets for close range target acquisition. All pictures in this section show models which can be seen in the Imperial War Museum, London.